"Prince Shakur's deft writing evoked a multi-layered emotional reaction almost immediately when I began reading. He writes from a place of honesty that is both searing and poignant in its transparency. His story will resonate deeply for those who hold hidden stories of sadness and grief tightly behind a smiling public mask."

—KHADIJAH ALI-COLEMAN

"*When They Tell You to Be Good* is a swirl of indelible images, language, and action that adds up to a daring coming-of-age memoir unbound by chronological time. Here, Prince Shakur insists on the irreducability of history, family, masculinity, race, identity, and geography. He refuses to allow manufactured borders between political, personal, and spiritual storytelling. This beautiful, antic, and deeply felt book makes the claim that love is not an emotion as much as it is a large and mysterious storm, encompassing deep pain and unbearable gulfs, yet always reaching for attachment and understanding. I love the anarchic confidence with which Shakur claims visionary thinkers and writers right alongside the people in his neighborhood, his family, friends, and comrades as his intellectual and emotional companions, establishing intimate, playful, heartbreaking, and powerful connections across all boundaries. I know we will be hearing much more from this irrepressible new literary voice."

—MADELINE FFITCH, author of *Stay and Fight*

"*When They Tell You to Be Good* is as inspiring as it is detailed. Being a gay, classified black male in America is not easy. Prince Shakur and I first crossed paths when I presented him with an award from GLAAD, but reading about Prince's shared but different experience made me feel the steps, levels and the purpose of the journey; handling love and abuse and learning that there can be a thin line between both. 'Would you care if I was gay?' is a question many members of the LGBTQIA+ family ask ourselves every day, whether to the bus driver or our father. Prince also intelligently explores the complicated yet straightforward relationship many men of all colors deal with: the subject of race."

—ZEKE THOMAS

"In *When They Tell You to Be Good*, Prince Shakur attempts to make sense of being born into, flung into, both the maw of American violence and the legendary lures and pressures of Babylon. While reckoning with the history of the murders of family members in Jamaica alongside the American state's history of murdering its Black beings, Prince charts a path through his queerness, his family history, films, literature, the Black radical tradition, as well as his own twin cultures, until an activist, a rigorously-fought-for sense of morality, and the contours of a lucid self comes into view. *This is how I've come to locate myself in time and space and legacy,* Prince seems to say, while unraveling a map of his own life. With *When They Tell You to Be Good*'s evergreen pairing of both finesse and confidence, it's miraculous to witness Prince assert that he is his own best cartographer."

—BERNARD FERGUSON

WHEN THEY TELL YOU TO BE GOOD

WHEN THEY TELL YOU TO BE GOOD

TO BE GOOD

A MEMOIR

PRINCE SHAKUR

TIN HOUSE / Portland, Oregon

Published by Tin House, Portland, Oregon

Distributed by W. W. Norton & Company

Library of Congress Cataloging-in-Publication Data

Names: Shakur, Prince, 1994- author.
Title: When they tell you to be good : a memoir / Prince Shakur.
Description: Portland, Oregon : Tin House, [2022]
Identifiers: LCCN 2022020914 | ISBN 9781953534422 (hardcover) | ISBN 9781953534507 (ebook)
Subjects: LCSH: Shakur, Prince, 1994- | Jamaican Americans--Biography. | African American gay men--Biography. | African American political activists--Biography. | United States--Race relations.
Classification: LCC E184.J27 S53 2022 | DDC 305.896/972920730092 [B]--dc23/eng/20220525
LC record available at https://lccn.loc.gov/2022020914

First US Edition 2022
Printed in the USA
Interior design by Jakob Vala

www.tinhouse.com

To Crystal, James Baldwin, KL Burd, Steven Yeager,
and every little kid writing towards a dream

Athens, Ohio, United States, 2014

I was nineteen years old and traveling cross-country when my mother told me that I'd die soon, like a man lunging out of a car and away from attackers. I stood in the antique shop in Montana, frozen by the cracking sound in my chest. It was the second time in five years that my mother brandished my father's murder, like a long and rusted machete. Is a mother's heartbreak worse than the heartbreak she gives her son?

Her words on that phone call rose a dark omen that said, "Your exodus means you are doomed. The great duppy will come for you, will chew you up like it got him." I spent weeks of that summer refusing my mother's calls. I only called my mother when my best friend from high school, Nadia, let me know more news about her mother, Crystal.

Nadia and I met when I considered myself a bookish, too-shy freshman, which was a world away from the college student drinking malt liquor at house shows that I'd become. We sat next to each other during our second year of high school, laughing on the phone after class as we watched yaoi anime on our laptops. Shortly after I came out at fifteen, my sobbing mother called Crystal for advice on how to grapple with having a gay son. It was Nadia and her family's acceptance of me that made living through the hell of my mother's homophobic reaction more bearable. At Nadia's house, I could talk about crushes on boys, while at my own home I wouldn't dare.

Weeks after coming out, Nadia accompanied my mother to help me move into a two-week summer workshop for teen writers. I lost my dorm key before they left. My mother and Nadia helped me search. My mother's nose burned brighter shades of red as we searched for my key for an hour. Her eyes flickered across all the white faces. Her embarrassment reached a fever pitch when she screamed at me in a bookstore as I searched. Heads around us turned in surprise.

Nadia eyed me and understood the double meaning in my mother's outburst. She stepped forward, touched my mother's arm, and whispered, "Ms. Shakur, we're calm. We're not freaking out. It's okay."

Nadia and her family bearing witness to my familial turmoil, even if it was from the periphery, calmed some of my feelings of abandonment. Through our senior year, I helped Nadia cope with her parents' divorce. We debated our college prospects after class, went to prom, and finalized our dorm packing lists together. While I skimmed by in classes and started to party, Nadia transferred universities and started to online date. Our collegiate phone calls became a needed check-in as we grappled with adulthood and how it changed the way we related to our parents.

I learned during the spring semester of my junior year that Crystal was battling stage 4 lung cancer. The mobile and cantankerous woman became bedridden and unable to eat many foods.

My mother, a hairstylist who had cancer patients before, helped Crystal look for wigs, connected her with a local resource center for cancer patients, and even invited a priest to her bedside.

My mother, a very introverted woman, savored her role as Crystal's caregiving friend. However proud I could be of my mother's tenderness from afar as I attended classes, it all perplexed me—the many promises my mother made to Crystal to look out for her daughter, the piousness in my mother's voice whenever she brought up how God brought her to Crystal, and how all the pain solidified her belief in a forgiving God who could offer spiritual relief to people in their last days. A God that had been weaponized against me.

During my fall semester of my junior year, which was before I learned of Crystal's cancer, my mother called and demanded to know how many people I'd come out to. She eventually revealed that my cousin, Anthony, was spreading the news of my sexuality. When my mother told me that she confronted him, it hurt the most to know that she'd said to him, "You can't be saying these bad things about my son."

Her version of defending me bothered me so much that I called her after a week of avoiding her and sank to the basement floor of my college house in defeat. I asked if she would ever be willing to understand my sexuality. My mother replied, "It's not in me. That's something I'll never want to understand. It hurts my heart, makes it hard to sleep at night. You understand?"

If even death couldn't sway my mother to love me more clearly, then what could shift the scales? What could bring us closer together as death, the only certain thing in life, inched closer and closer?

A year later during my fall semester as a senior, Nadia sent me a text while I was in a meeting—"My mother died an hour ago." Reading the words that Crystal had died hollowed out an unexpected place in me. I stumbled into the hallway, tried to decide what to text her back, and called my mother.

"What do I do? Should I buy a bus ticket home right now? Does she need my help?"

My mother thought for a moment, "Wait until the funeral is announced. Give her a little time to tell you what to do."

I hung up the phone, reached for my swelling throat, and started to cry. The kind of crying that tore through a stomach, sprinkled jagged glass there, and stitched it back together again. I couldn't get enough of the water out of my chest, so the coughing and near gagging began. At twenty years old, I was just starting my life and now death was framing it, moving in closer and closer.

In August 2014, a month before Crystal died in her hospital bed, a Black teenager was walking home with his friend. They stopped at a gas station and the tall Black teenager bought a few things from the store. As he and his friend jaywalked, a cop arrived and allegedly ordered them to leave the street. Michael Brown was shot six times. Hours later, his body lay still in the street and the nearby crowds grew larger. His murder and display was a harkening to Nina Simone's "Strange Fruit," a song that Nina Simone said was unappealing, in a certain sense, and whose namesake became the title of a 2017 documentary on Brown's effective lynching. Black people, once again, had to choose how to deal with America's torture and how to reclaim our dead.

■ ■ ■

The funeral home was small and not far from where my mother lived. We walked through the maze of cars in the parking lot to the open front door. My mother spent most of the morning and the night before on the phone, talking about Crystal's decline to friends. I wanted to be supportive to her and listen, but it irked me when she said things like, "I think God really wanted me to help. I learned a lot about myself through helping her."

My mother believed that God or the devil placed horrible things in your path to test your faith, which to me meant that Crystal's sickness served some high power. Good people suffer to bring empathy to the world. This belief seemed like an easy way out of my mother being vulnerable enough to acknowledge the terror of Crystal's demise to me. I wanted to scream that pain did not equal faith. Even in my anger, I buried my words because everything about the world was moving too fast. Knots collected in my stomach as I hugged Nadia's brother and father. A few minutes before the service started, my mother leaned toward me.

"Did I ever tell you about one of the last times I saw her?"

"Um . . ." I sighed. "No."

"I visited her in the hospital. She started coughing and coughing. Then she started coughing up blood with *things* in it."

I tried to look ahead and not respond to my mother. A thousand things raced through my head: whether to tell her to shut up, whether to slap her across the face, or how to blink away the heat rushing to my eyes. I wanted the version of my mother that helped my brother make the miniature volcano for a science fair on the kitchen floor, who bought me McDonald's after nosebleeds in elementary school, and who stood between the world and my brother and me when I was twelve. Now my mother stared at me and kissed her teeth.

"You've had an attitude all morning and now you're not talking to me."

I excused myself to the bathroom. A man stood at the counter counting his pills in a pill dispenser. I locked myself in a stall and wondered why the fuck he was there. I shook my head repeatedly and told myself that it was too early to cry. Then the image crossed my mind. Blood and body parts leaving Crystal's lips, her face pinched in pain. I wanted a different image. More than anything, I wanted to be walking into Crystal's living room with a soda in hand and a laughing Nadia at my side, or for that image to be burned into my mind.

The service was well enough. The funeral director was an older Black man that sometimes stumbled over his words. He said all of the expected things after someone's passing, especially on how one's life can be measured by how much they moved people. Nadia walked out in a beautiful black dress with her brother by her side. They sat at the front. Not being able to read the emotions on Nadia's face terrified me. I wished that I was sitting right next to her. I was angry that I didn't have the courage to speak at the wake about what Crystal meant to me out of fear that the true face of my grief would offend my mother. I wanted to stay longer at the end, but my mother rushed us away and said that our presence wouldn't be helpful.

I stared out the window during the short drive home and loosened my tie.

"I'm going to my room," I said as soon as we got back.

I tried to take a nap. I didn't feel like scrolling through my phone. I didn't feel like texting or calling anyone, and I didn't want to cry. Eventually, my phone buzzed. It was Nadia.

"Can you help me pack up my mother's room tonight?"

"Of course I can. I'll get my mother to drop me off."

I opened my bedroom door and found my mother in the kitchen. I asked if she could take me to Nadia's house.

"If I drop you off there, then how are you going to get to the bus to go back to school tomorrow?"

My mother turned off the kitchen faucet and left the half-filled pot in the sink. Then she turned to me slowly. My older brother was back home to eat a home-cooked dinner. She was hoping that we would all sit together and reminisce about how much Crystal had meant to us, or more specifically, to her. I chose my words carefully.

"Nadia really needs help right now. Tonight's gonna be hard because she has to clear out her mother's room. Her father isn't there. Her brother isn't there. I—"

"So you need to be there?"

If you were actually Crystal's actual friend, maybe you'd be going there too, I thought.

I knew what was coming—the sometimes pained twinkle in her eye whenever I talked about how fun Crystal was, how threatened my mother felt over my level of ease with Crystal's family, and how this could mean that I, in turn, didn't care enough to understand my mother. Pretty soon, all the hurt bubbling beneath the surface would all come flying out of my mouth. My heart started to race. I bit down on the inside of my lip. Through the fresh, hot grief in my mind, I stared at myself standing in a little vintage shop in Wyoming, trying to imagine the horrible things my father had done to make my mother curse me to death. I was staring at my mother peel open Crystal's door to find her on the ground. I was watching my mother use her religion to rationalize everything, even pushing me away by demanding I be something that I wasn't. I was waiting for her God to bring Crystal back. I wanted to scream.

I had dared to hope that Crystal's passing would somehow bring my mother and me closer together, that death would even us out on the same plateau of grief. Instead, it revealed the ways we used love and loyalty differently. For me, Crystal's death was the equivalent of an anchor's rope being cut. To my mother, her death was proof of God's willingness to have mercy on those capable of change and devotion.

I spoke with a clear voice, "Her mother, your friend, died today."

"And I haven't seen you, my son, in months. Now you're going to hang out with your friend? Prince, I don't think you realize how selfish you are sometimes."

I turned away. She shouted, "You can find your own ride to the bus tomorrow."

I spun around and walked toward her, then stopped saying, "I knew you would do this. I knew you would do this. Nadia's mother has been sick for over a year. You swoop in and pretend like you have this big heart. I'll find my own way to the bus station tomorrow, but it's really sick for you to make today about you."

"Shoot me for wanting to see my son."

"You don't care about your son. If you cared, you would have noticed why I didn't talk to you for a month this past summer. You don't know anything about my life."

I rushed to my room, grabbed my bag, and started to fling things inside. I texted Nadia, apologizing and asking her to pick me up. I waited in my room with my bag. If I could last another ten minutes, I would be out of this hellhole. A knock came at my door. It was my brother. He was tall and dark and his eyebrows pinched together.

"You okay?"

I crossed my arms from where I sat on the floor. It seemed ridiculous that he was asking me if I was okay. He'd never checked in with me during Crystal's sickness or my summer away. Before I could respond, my mother pushed open the door from behind him.

"If you didn't wanna visit, you shouldn't have. You should have stayed with another one of your friends instead of coming here and using this bed."

In all the horror of Crystal's passing, I couldn't get a memory from when I was a child out of my head. I was a toddler in Jamaica with my mother and uncle when we went to the beach. My uncle Senel, with his large Black hands, led me out to the water and told me he'd teach me how to swim. What started as a gentle bobbing up and down turned into a violent heaving of my body with his large hands moving me up and down and up and down into the water as I screamed, cried, and laughed. The entire time, my mother sat on the shore watching from beneath her straw hat until I collapsed onto the sand next to her. She'd said, "They used to do that to me too."

It was the first time that I could remember my mother not showing up for me. Trying to lick my wounds, I tucked this memory to the back of my mind only to realize as an adult that maybe it was telling me something Not all children have the luxury of total safety with their parents. Sometimes emotional survival meant fighting back.

"You are not a good person," I said to my mother as she stood in the doorway. "You're not a Christian. You talked so much about how much Crystal meant to you and how many promises you made her. Why did you latch onto a dying woman? Why was that so easy for you?"

A shiver moved through me as both my mother's and brother's eyes shot up. Our mother's loud curses fell over my ears. My brother shot his arms out to block my mother from coming at me through the open doorway.

I shouted over her, "I don't come home more because you like playing the part of a mother. You talk down to your children. You never apologize. I avoid you because I don't need you to make Nadia's mother dying about you! I loved her too."

The air left the room and I felt dizzy. Something took over our bodies, morphing us into monsters more concerned with hurting each other than with Crystal's passing. My screaming, I realized, was my way of setting fire to my mother's illusions, which surrounded her like walls, forever unable to see my pain.

Nadia arrived outside. I rushed out the front door, slinging my bag over my shoulder as my mother yelled behind me. I was so upset, but refused to cry, even once I was safe and Nadia drove away. Nadia glanced at me a few good times and didn't say anything.

"Your mother is a trip, huh?" she finally said.

I laughed. I tried to smile at her, but I couldn't. I hated the thought that Crystal would be displeased with me in this moment. For the next two hours, we went through her mother's room, sorted papers, and tried to tidy up as many artifacts of Crystal's life. I palmed Crystal's medical bills and mail as I fought back tears, knowing that I'd done the same for my stepfather only a few years before, after his arrest. How many times would Black children be left with the wreckage, whether large or small, of their parent's lives?

It neared midnight when I found Nadia in the kitchen. For the past two hours, I'd snuck glimpses at Nadia and wondered why no one else in her family was here to help. Though she'd alluded to the more estranged nature of her mother's side of the family, it still floored me to see their material absence on this dark night of Nadia's soul. What was family for if they didn't face the darkness with you? I poured myself a glass of water from the kitchen faucet. We leaned against the counters and looked at each other.

"How do you feel?" I asked.

She looked small in the darkness as she wore her gray sweats. I tried to think of how different we looked only five years before, after meeting as high school freshmen in a hallway. I, painfully shy, and she, always ready to burst with laughter as her love helped me rebirth myself. I only wished I could do the same for her. She shrugged in response.

"None of it makes any sense. I was just sitting there and realizing that this was it. Someone is gonna have to take care of this house and the bills. I feel like I'm drowning, but I don't know what drowning is supposed to feel like."

We sank down to sit on the floor. It was night, but the moon wasn't very large, so the kitchen was dim. I waited for a few moments and then nodded.

"But you have Guru, right?"

A small smile crossed her face. She had been dating Guru for over a year. It was beautiful to see my best friend be the first of the two of us to date. Guru was tall and overzealous about his affection for Nadia. Sometimes I worried that he was too invested in her, but I could only be thankful that their relationship had helped her get to this very moment. Nadia wiped at her face.

"And how are you? You think you gonna talk to your mother anytime soon?"

I didn't want to cry, but I also didn't like the question.

"I don't know honestly," I replied and felt my stomach tense. "I haven't been this angry in such a long time. I've been through so many things this past year. We have been through so many things this past year and I kind of hoped that all of this would soften her. I just worry . . ."

I let my voice trail off, too afraid to say what I really wanted to, which was that I always feared that the next argument with my mother would be my final leap of faith into a life potentially devoid of the person that had brought me into the world.

"She did love my mother though and help her, which I appreciate," Nadia said. "Your mom visited my mother a lot. Talked to her, and tried to give her some peace. Sometimes I heard them talking about you. Your mom was always saying how worried about you she was. My mom just told your mom to calm down, to realize you're not running these streets, and that you're doing good things."

I wanted to be strong enough to believe that Crystal's acceptance would nudge my mother to learn how to love me better, but the truth was that Crystal's death had decimated that hope, which now felt childish. The forbidden thing was that I grieved Nadia's mother in a way that I wasn't sure that I would grieve my own. I sometimes thought of the day that my own mother would pass, how I'd be an orphan, flung out into the universe in one last, painful act of being set free from the expectations of being born to parents that didn't know how to love this version of me. And how, in some ways, I didn't want to be set free because it meant that I would have to accept death, along with the love and pain and violence that had preceded it.

I wanted life to be easy on us. But just like the reckoning that Black America was experiencing at this time, I had to decide just how much pain I could handle for the sake of progress.

■ ■ ■

I returned to my senior year after Crystal's funeral to the continued mayhem of the Blood Bucket Challenge. Since the start of the year, I'd joined Student Senate as a member of the LGBTQIA Affairs Commission after helping canvass for the Restart Student Ticket the previous year. I'd met Megan Marzec, the current Student Senate president, the year before. She was an art major with long black hair and an observant, yet metered gaze. She ran on radical policies, won, and when challenged by the university president, Roderick McDavis, to the ALS Ice Bucket Challenge, Megan responded politically.

While on camera, she dumped a bucket of fake blood onto herself and demanded that our university divest from companies with ties to Israel in solidarity with the international Boycott, Divest, and Sanction campaign. The past summer of Israel bombing the Gaza Strip had surely made international news, but as far as the white, liberal college students were concerned, it was seldom a topic of discussion.

Our school's newspapers filled with more headlines about "the Blood Bucket Challenge" as the days passed. I heard whispers that the FBI recommended that Megan accept their protective services. Around campus, it was easy to fall into arguments with other students about how inappropriate the drasticness of Megan's political action had been or how she had done something controversial, but most students seldom talked about the measure of human life at stake, especially for those in the Gaza Strip and Palestine. Shortly after the video of Megan went online, Ohio University released a statement in response:

> The role and value of a higher education institution is to foster civil discussions about important and complex issues. To be sure, the Student Senate president in her video altered the original spirit with which President Roderick J. McDavis issued the ALS Ice Bucket Challenge. Her [Megan Marzec's] actions do not reflect the position of Ohio University or President McDavis. We recognize the rights of individual students to speak out on matters of public concern and we will continue to do so, but want to be clear that the message shared today

by her is not an institutional position or a belief held by President McDavis.

For so much of my college career, I was used to simply adjusting to collegiate life or trying to shrug off my straightedge tendencies from high school. Meeting friends who campaigned for the Restart Student Ticket and who organized in the Ohio University Student Union showed me another side of campus, where boys with dangly earrings drank next to veterans in dive bars, where people read bad poetry to each other onstage, and somehow in the structured freedom of it all, where we found new ways to act politically.

At the beginning of my senior year, before death took Crystal, I went to New York City with the Student Union for a two-mile march called the People's Climate March. It was supposed to be one of the largest environmental marches to date with an ambiguous political mission of saving the environment. The advertisements and billboards glowed in Time Square. I slept in the basement of a church, roamed the city, and for the first time in a while, could move through an hour without thinking of Crystal.

I became closer to Olivia around that time. Olivia was shorter, with tan skin, and spoke with softness and reverence. She visited Ferguson days before fall semester started and came back to Athens, Ohio, inspired. She morphed from the person that rejected a boy I liked the year before into a conduit to the events, fires, and tear gas canisters showering down in Ferguson. I met her on College Green on the first day of classes after seeing a Facebook event for a sit-in.

White students milled around us as usual. Some eyed the signs that were being painted. Others scoffed as they passed. I sat down, talked to Olivia about the way that the news was representing the protests, and was struck by her urgency. She said, "There's no point in us just watching the news. If this is something that a lot of people care about, shouldn't we do more than watch?"

I was taken back to being at the side of my stepfather, Dennis, as he watched the news or slumbered on the couch. Those childhood memories of him debating news events with his friends showed me that it was okay for men to be curious and challenge the assumptions of those around him.

If there was anything that the internet age had brought us, it was the ability to bear witness to the emptiness of American culture or be drowned by the existential impossibility of it; bloated Black bodies floating along the waters of New Orleans, slim figures on a camera clinging onto the windows of the World Trade Center as smoke billowed out—all warlike images burned into the cultural imagination.

"So you want to make this feel more real for people?" I asked. She nodded.

The group of about a dozen of us grabbed signs and marched around campus. In Baker Student Center, other students openly gawked. The sparse onlooker glared at a sign that read, "Black Lives Matter," twisted their face in shock, and yelled, "Read all the facts."

My face grew hot. I tried to not sweat as we walked on. Once we got back to College Green, back to our classes, and on to our normal days, I couldn't shake this new feeling that white people's eyes were always the metaphorical cameras to our misery; only now those cameras surrounded me at all times, re-fracting the very idea that I could meet my end at any moment.

The next day, a photo of me on College Green ended up on the front page of *The Post*. In it, I am wearing gray slacks and a black polo shirt, and am holding up a sign that says "Black Life. Any Life Should Matter" as I stare at the camera. Look-ing back at the photo a few years later, I recognize a new kind of determination in my face, one that was ready to see how far Black people would have to go to take ourselves out of a world that could so easily destroy us.

This determination made it easy for me to make deeper connections with the students of color around me. A few weeks later, Olivia texted a contact list of people who'd shown up to her rally to inform us that an organizer conference call would be happening soon with people from Ferguson. Intrigued, I walked to Olivia's house on the west side of Athens. I arrived to find Kelli eating chips at the dining room table, her curly bangs shaking as she laughed at Olivia's joke.

I'd known Kelli since freshman year, but we had never really been friends. The year before I'd tagged along with her and her friends to a party. I'd watched as they danced and laughed, still feeling like the straightedge freshman too scared to buy alcohol underage at the one shop in town that didn't card. As college went on, Kelli and I gravitated to a lot of the same spaces and parties with people that liked poetry, moshing around in a living room, or getting drunk on PBR. Now our spaces had become more political.

■ ■ ■

The conference call warned that a verdict on the cop who killed Michael Brown would happen in the coming weeks. There would be a weekend of political events and rallies in Ferguson with a goal of bringing his murder to people's doorsteps.

We were members of the Student Senate and could present a resolution to use a small amount of the student government's budget to fund travel to Ferguson.

On the car ride to Ferguson, I stuck to my resolve to not tell my mother that I was traveling. Her venomous overreaction over my bus mishap the summer before on my way to Yellowstone had stayed with me. I didn't want her to lecture me about getting distracted in the eleventh hour of college.

We stayed with a white woman named Sarah that lived in the suburbs and offered up space to visiting protesters. Sarah's home was ornate with a dark-wood staircase that met you in the foyer and numerous empty rooms. She had been a part of an action a few weeks earlier where protesters disrupted the St. Louis Symphony. On our first morning in St. Louis, we gathered in Sarah's kitchen. She gave us food to eat for the day, then pulled me aside.

"I know I'm a white woman and I know this whole experience is probably a lot for you, but I wouldn't be honest if I didn't tell you one thing," she said. "The news is trying to vilify Black men that are at these protests. If something serious goes down and you're wearing a bandana to cover your face from tear gas and your photo ends up in the news . . ."

Sarah slid a copy of the newspaper toward me. The front-page photo was of a Black man in khaki pants masked up as he fled a crowd. The headline was inflammatory and dismissive. I stared at her brown hair and dark eyes. Maybe it was the absence of Crystal or the fact that my own mother didn't know that I was here, but I felt keen to listen to Sarah, especially since I was in a new city and engaging in a political environment that wasn't my own. Her words shook me because they echoed those of so many other mothers that I'd met in my life: the women at my mother's shop that told me to stay in school, my aunts congratulating me on making the honor roll, or my mother warning me to not walk with my hoodie up or headphones on. Now I was in the starving belly of Black America as it fought once again for sustenance.

During the day, Kelli, Eli, Jasmine, and I walked in a massive rally that ended in a park. For most of the ride to St. Louis, Jasmine, another Black student in the Senate with us, was silent. I had spent many meetings with Jasmine and others from her political ticket as they sighed and rolled their eyes at the university policies, like opening up voting to all students, that my friends and I presented. When Kelli, Olivia, and I presented the idea of a trip to Ferguson to the Student Senate, we were pleasantly surprised when Jasmine expressed interest.

Eli, a friend and student journalist accompanying us, sprinted around, snapping photos and constantly leaving our line of sight, despite the fact that we agreed to stick together. He joined the trip as a student photojournalist that was keen on getting images of the emerging movement.

I first noticed Eli during my sophomore year of college for his tanned skin and tight facial features. At a karaoke event in Baker Center, he wore cargo shorts and a basic T-shirt, and had shaggy hair, but something about his demeanor was confident and comforting. He belted out an '80s rock song among a sea of pop renditions. He often biked around campus, his powerful legs turning the pedals, chains, and wheels. I struggled through a human geography class that I signed up for to fulfill a science credit and gawked at how smoothly he answered any question after raising his hand in class. The most troubling part of the class was the weekly geography quiz we had to take, which I always failed. While looking for a table in the library to study at, my classmate and I noticed Eli, then looked at each other.

"I think he could help us study," I mumbled.

My classmate tried to shrug nonchalantly, but her face had an edge of hope. I walked over, desperate, as I introduced myself to him.

He smirked at me and said, "You're the dude that shows up to class late all the time, right?"

I froze and tried to think of a response. He laughed. Our friendship moved from that library study session to me complaining to him about the difficulty of finding a summer job in Athens. He invited me to his house in the early summer after I moved into my house on North Lancaster on the town's west side. After cooking lunch, we walked along a nearby bike path. He asked why I never talked about dating anyone. My heart raced as I told him that I was gay and that dating in college was difficult.

"Hm. I never thought of that before, but that must be true," he replied.

I was stunned by his casualness at my sexuality, or more specifically, how unthreatened he was in a world that taught men to feel threatened all the time. I admired Eli's passion for his major and how rationally he pursued his goals. Eli's house and talkative mother became a life raft for me as I navigated my family problems, similar to how Crystal's home nurtured me.

I texted him after I found out that Nadia's mother had died. "What do you want to do?" he texted back as I sat sobbing in Baker Center. Then he called and all he could hear on my line was uncontrollable crying as I tried to say hello. I told him that the only thing I really wanted to do was to hang out at his house. I walked ten minutes across town.

On a side street, he jumped off of his bike, found me wiping my face, and gave me a hug. In the midst of Michael Brown's death and as America started to feel like it was opening up beneath our feet, people like Eli helped me realize that we should trust the people that will be there when our world, whether personal or collective, implodes.

Now we all stood at the fountain in the park in St. Louis, which had water dyed red as a decoration for a baseball game. Jasmine shook her head and Kelli put an arm around her shoulder. Eli took a photo of two young Black boys as they sat in front of the fountain. Goose bumps along my arm sent a shiver down my spine.

Eli said what we were all thinking. "It looks like blood."

The day moved on as the march concluded with a series of speeches. We rushed on over to a gathering in front of Canfield Apartments, where Michael Brown was shot and killed.

We passed by homes on the walk to the Ferguson Police Department as we filled the streets. As the chants continued, I felt something else take the place of fear—pride. For the first time in my life, I was not afraid of how deeply I could be hurt because of the color of my skin. What began to matter more was the voracity at which I could love, how close I stayed to justice, and if I could give voice to the dead.

Men, women, and children opened their front doors and raised their fists in the air. Everyone that looked out at us was Black. These were the same people that had seen their neighborhoods turned into a war zone as Ferguson police swept through it, attempting to disperse protesters with batons and tear gas. I thought of the mothers who shooed their children inside of their houses or told them to lie on the floor as the chaos filled their neighborhoods. The history books in school had left this part out. The little nigger boys in the streets setting fires and looting businesses, their hearts could be in the revolution too. All of the busted-up women on the street corners with missing teeth, their deepest desires could be seen and respected too. No college degree was needed to shout Michael Brown's name. No degree of respectability could save us either. If we fought together, then our Blackness could mean far more than what we had been told it was our entire lives. I was Black. I was marching and if I went to jail, so be it. In the least, Michael Brown deserved an ounce of the dedication that I was just learning to give.

The crowd stopped in front of the Ferguson Police Department. A line of police in riot gear formed. Black teenagers and adults stood toe to toe with officers, spit flying from their mouths. A junker car blasted rap music. Among the anger, something else was brewing. The night was late, but the crowd swelled and pulsated. Another realization hit me. That something infecting the crowd was pride too.

When we got back to Athens, Kelli, Olivia, Jasmine, and I were determined to organize a protest that garnered all of the university's attention. In solidarity with the organizer of Ferguson October, we planned for a walkout at 12:01 p.m., the same time that Michael Brown was murdered, to be on a national day of action.

I started to move around campus differently. The sea of white faces in classes, in the dining halls, and at parties suddenly felt built on the carnage of everything beneath our feet and around us the whole time. Black death could not exist or be honored in spaces only meant for some Black people. And I had fallen into that very space. At a party, a white student introduced himself to me and told me that he had seen me canvassing around campus.

"I think these issues are important," he said close to my ear in a loud kitchen. "But getting angry won't make anyone want to listen to you. Those people rioting have to be strategic."

It was my first time talking to a white person who, when confronted with my reality of being Black in America, wanted to tell me how I should react to my own unraveling. I argued with him about how these protests were more than just protests to me, and tried to get him to understand that, for some people, being politically active meant risking death. I rushed upstairs, my body shaking. I was reminded of the hell of the Blood Bucket Challenge, of all the death threats that Megan had gotten, and how feverish people's support of the status quo was. I was beginning to realize that the response to the grief that America expected was platitudes about racial progress and civil conversations.

Kelli grabbed me when she found me sobbing on the second floor of the party, held my face, and said, "Don't let that white boy ruin your night."

The moment brought me back to my strongest memory of her. During my junior year at a party, I helped her walk a mutual friend back to his house as he drunkenly mused about suicide. She spoke to him softly and helped him decide to go to bed. She stood in his dark living room after he went to sleep, put her face into her hands, and cried. She cared about the world in a way that was recognizable to me.

We paired up to canvass sections for our upcoming protest and learned the best method was to walk along with a student and overwhelm them with information. "Have you heard about the police murder of Michael Brown? . . . Oh no? Well, this past August, a white police officer stopped a Black teen on his way home, shot him in cold blood, and now city prosecutors in St. Louis are deciding if he should be convicted for Michael Brown's murder. Even in an America with a Black president, a Black teen can be shot while walking home. Do you think more people should know about this?"

Kelli and I perfected our canvassing speeches, performed a die-in, pitched the walkout to Black student organizations, made banners, sent letters to the local newspapers, and set up a text alert service to notify students when to walk out of their classes. As the day of the action approached, my mind drifted to Crystal more. I had wanted the world to stop because she was gone. Now America was being forced to watch as its own people said a Black teenager's name again and again and again. Hands up. Don't shoot. Why did you do that, officer? I was just trying to walk home. My mother is waiting for me.

The walkout, by all means, was a success. It was the first political action of its kind during my time at Ohio University, one where students and faculty and others were asked to leave their normal schedule on a whim to leave a space, a gap, a silence to signify a loss. Numerous news outlets asked for interviews. We went from speeches to clenched fists in the air to my own words melting loudly into the audience when I said, "When my mother tells me that she wants me to be good and happy and strong and proud, I think of this."

Since Michael Brown's death in August, the Ferguson Police Department spent $172,000 dealing with protesters. On November 22, a Black boy in Cleveland was playing in a park with a BB gun when a police cruiser pulled up, the passenger door flung open. Tamir Rice, who was twelve years old and 5' 7", was dead. I began to understand that my home city was entangled with America's murder of Black boys like Tamir Rice and Emmett Till and of Black women at the hands of the Cleveland Strangler, a man named Anthony Sowell that kidnapped, assaulted, and murdered at least eleven women. Two days after Tamir Rice's death, Kelli suggested that Black students gather on College Green to hear the verdict against Darren Wilson, the police officer that shot and killed Michael Brown.

We gathered on College Green, bundled up in our coats to ward off the winter cold, and huddled around my cell phone as the announcement was made. We all stood, watching our breaths and each other's breaths, yet holding close to another part of ourselves that was waiting to breathe too, that was waiting to tell us our future.

...

Michael Brown was not the end. He was a rupture among many ruptures. By Christmas, we would deal with the matter of Eric Garner, harassed, attacked, and choked on video. Although the media purported large, Black men to be scary, I mostly thought of the many uncles I'd seen at barbecues growing up as they laughed, drank beer, and hugged their daughters tightly. Now suddenly gone. My friends and I clamored to react. I helped organize a demonstration where I challenged people to hold signs that said "I Can't Breathe" through their day. If white people were going to watch and be silent, I at least wanted to confront them with Eric Garner's words. For Black people, his last sputtered breaths were already ringing in our ears.

We gathered on the Athens Courthouse steps. Jasmine cried, grieving into a megaphone a basic truth—she, like so many other Black people, was tired. It started to rain and an eerie juxtaposition arose as we blocked traffic, shouted, and marched as Christmas music played. During a die-in on the first floor of the university president's office, a Black professor looked over our bodies jammed together on the floor.

"Remember the slave ships," she said. "Remember what your ancestors survived. The shit and piss and smell and darkness."

I boarded a plane to Costa Rica with Eli in December and spent the holidays with him and his mother. We cooked rice and refried beans on their small stove at their house in Orosi

Valley. Sometimes I walked to the store a half a mile from their house, marveled at the mountains, and bought beef empanadas that melted in my mouth with each bite. I devoured *The New Jim Crow* by Michelle Alexander all while thinking of the words that I heard a Black teen say in the Ferguson Commonique video. He said, "I want a better forever. A better tomorrow will not save me."

On Christmas, Eli and I got drunk with his friends. I fell asleep in the town's main plaza, my belly filled with too much Four Loko. The longer the trip lasted, the more I dove into myself because I was unable to speak Spanish. Entire dinners passed where I said no more than a few sentences. If I could hold a sign with Eric Garner's words and remain invisible on my campus, then what did it mean to feel invisible in another place and context?

Even in Costa Rica, I couldn't shake thoughts of Crystal mainly because I didn't want to. In the dim and quaint living room of Eli's mother's house, I watched a film late at night where a girl fades into cancer's delirium. Just before she dies, she has one last lucid moment of sitting in her dining room, staring at her younger brother playing in the backyard, and wondering, "Is this really it?"

I sobbed through the credits. I wondered if Crystal had ever been granted that kind of serenity near the end, if my mother had helped her, or if she'd be angry with me for how confused her passing had left me. The cloud of grief was pushing me toward something that I didn't understand or wasn't ready for. How many of us were walking around with our bellies, hearts, and minds filled with all of the people that we'd lost, the people we had yet to lose?

I tagged along with Eli and his romantic fling to a club in Monte Verde. The dance floor billowed with fog as he and that short beautiful girl swayed to the salsa music. I watched as couples danced, wondering how to untangle momentary longing for a friend, like Eli, from the grief of being a world away from my home, Ohio, where Crystal was born, lived, raised a family, had given so much to a Black boy like me, and was now gone. I ran back to the place where we were staying in a nauseated blur. Something had to change, so I told Eli the next morning, "Can your friend give me a tattoo?"

It was a week or so later when I walked into the bedroom of his friend, Carlos, and told him my tattoo idea. He placed the sketch on my back as I leaned into a chair. Everyone in the room spoke in Spanish, but even that didn't matter. I melted into the pain, or better yet, the pain melted into me. When the hours were done, I stood in a weary state. I couldn't make out the full piece in the mirror, so Eli took a picture and showed me. On my back was the Black power fist clutching a chain with one of the links broken.

Someone had fed into Michael Brown and Eric Garner, just as someone had fed into me. It was strange to think, but whatever heaven they existed in, I knew that they could be trudging alongside Crystal as she looked down at Nadia and me. If by some chance, she stumbled into a man that was tall and lean and handsome and tanned by the same sun shining down on Jamaica, she could look at him and say, "You love them too, huh?"

They would look down on us and I hoped that they would look with the same reverence in their gaze I'd seen after I climbed into my mother's car four years ago. It was the day of college move-in my freshman year. I stared out the window and watched as Nadia's house and the foliage in the front yard shrank as we pulled away. I kept my gaze fixed on Crystal with Nadia at her side. Crystal's hand was high in the air, waving and waving and her mouth in a wide grin, still crying, still wishing me well, always wishing me well.

There was so much hate in the world, but there was also so much love as long as I could find it. Beneath the tattoo on my back read the words, "For the ones I love, I will sacrifice."

Sacrifice. There was a lot of that in the world too.

Montego Bay, Jamaica, 1962–present day

In the videotape of the joint funeral of my uncles, Senel and Derrick, a faint scream can be heard in the background from outside of the church. My mother returned home with the tape from Jamaica and told me that the scream had been her when she'd walked outside. In the hot March sun, she'd keeled over in her dress and wailed; something about the image of her motionless brothers and what couldn't escape her still gives me shivers to this day. With her scream, I assumed my mother was trying to banish the horror of their murders, all of the murky darkness around it, and the evils of Babylon away. We are raised on the notion that family can save us, so it hurts when we cannot save them.

Senel's and Derrick's murders left visible devastation in their wake. Family members regularly visited and fed my grandmother, who lived alone. Everyone spent hours on the phone tracking down the bodies, arranging autopsies, and preparing them for the funeral. In the coming weeks, my mother, a woman who often prided herself on being proactive, became a ghost. She returned home and lay in her bedroom as my brother and I amused ourselves downstairs. She sat at the table with us when dinner was ready and cried over glasses of wine. She cried when she dropped us off at school and thanked us for cleaning the house. The loss had happened. But something deep in our family and my mother was actively rupturing. Grief's laser focus made me aware of this.

■ ■ ■

In Rastafarianism, Babylon is considered the man-made governments and institutions that go against Jah (or God). As Rastafarianism developed as an ideology, Babylon became symbolic of Western and white society, which has worked to enslave and exploit Afro-diaspora people. Politricksters are all politicians who trick the citizens they are presumed to govern with lies and fallacies. The police execute Babylon's will.

For years, I heard the term "Babylon" used in Jamaican music and cinema, but never thoroughly understood what it meant. I assumed the word would eventually define itself. But I was wrong in the sense that when we are born, we are born into someone else's history, someone else's memory. The living embody the dead. This mere fact means that we must do more than stumble into our lives, upon our histories, answers, and ideologies. We must search and question to find meaning. What we are handed is not always what we must take.

■ ■ ■

On that February evening in 2006, a group of men went into the home of my uncles on Felicity Road in Montego Bay,

Jamaica. My uncles had found the money for supplies and had been building their large cement mansion for a number of years. The lower floors were gutted and a maze of exposed rods.

I spent a lot of the days in the summer before their murders at their house, playing hide-and-seek with Derrick's son, who was my age. We sat inside the living room with white linoleum tile and watched old martial arts movies on hot days. If the heat snuck into the evening, my uncles peeled off their shirts, and their dark skin glistened like blades of dewy grass. Senel or Derrick would bring us bag juice and instruct us on how to grow up to be decent, non-womanizing men. At the end of that summer, I sat on the phone with my mother in their house as she told me I'd be going to a new middle school. I later realized Senel and Derrick were killed thirty minutes from where I'd sat on the phone.

"Whoever killed them must have used a silencer as we never heard any shots being fired," said a neighbor who lived in the downstairs section of my uncles' home to the *Jamaica Gleaner* in 2006. "I slept here Wednesday night and last night and I didn't hear anything unusual."

There is significance in how the most enduring lessons I can remember Senel and Derrick imparting to me was how to not hurt or be hurt by a woman. The third member of the triple murder was Senel's girlfriend. To this day, I still wonder how men can find the language to articulate how they've hurt others, what that hurt leaves behind, and how we can survive without our tenderness destroyed.

Even at ten years old as I left their home for the last time before their murders, it dawned on me that their advice couldn't work for every boy becoming a man, which meant that maybe it didn't work for me. A group of men went into their home, forced three people to lie on the ground, and shot them in the back of their heads. Felicity Road lived up to its nickname, Blood Lane.

In a 2006 article, the Jamaican superintendent John Morris described Senel and Derrick Taylor as "no angels," with "extensive criminal records" in the US. He alluded to the fact that their murders were "ordered by criminal elements in the United States with strong links to the criminal underworld in Montego Bay." His rationale transformed the slain into long-time criminals that had just gotten their bit of karma.

My uncles exist in the foggy eye of my childhood's memory. I knew they liked Red Stripe beer and Peter Tosh. Derrick's wedding photos adorned our family's living room in Cleveland. Senel and Derrick would hug my mother with force, and were of the few people that could tease her to the point of laughter. When I read "no angels," I think of Michael Brown, all of the other large, murdered Black men to come, and the fear required to turn a man into a monster that must be slayed. I think of my mother's scream, how the church couldn't even attempt to contain it, and what the world creates for people to be born into, live through, and die in. Just as Assata Shakur noted that revolutionaries do not fall from the moon, I say that my uncles were born as demons ripping into the world.

In a country like Jamaica, how does the labeling of men, like my uncles, as "no angels" minimize the structural, political, and patriarchal violence that molded them? When the living or dead become objectively criminal, we neglect to examine how

Babylon and the forces of Western society have succeeded or failed in creating outlaws and revolutionaries. A just society empowers people to oppose the institutions that have failed or exploited them with the help of education and resources. An unjust society pulls the wool over our eyes, profits off of our misery, enables institutions to disenfranchise us, and uses our death to further a narrative that justifies more control. The men of my family and of the Afro-Caribbean diaspora are products of masculinities crafted by an unjust society. They lived and died in a world that could have saved them, but didn't. They are survived by many people who struggle to make sense of their violence.

Masculinity is a social construct. It is a set of traits, behaviors, and roles associated with boys, men, or people with penises. In Raewyn Cowell's *Masculinities*, Cowell makes many vital distinctions about masculinity. Numerous masculinities exist and can be produced within the same setting. Violence among men is often transactional and a means of asserting their gender. This logic is how I could go from the scorned gay Black boy in school to earning the respect of my peers by "standing up" for myself or playing along with the charade of heteronormativity. Masculinity also shifts in response to cultural events.

From this framework, Jamaican masculinities are the product of the island's history, which is marked by colonialism, slavery, the struggle for independence from Britain, political/gang violence, and drug culture. From the genocide of roughly 85 percent of the Arawak indigenous population in the 1500s following the arrival of Spanish/British colonizers to Xaymaca, the hierarchy of slave men and women during plantation slavery, the economic decline of the island following its independence from

37

Britain in 1962, and subsequent violence of Jamaican political parties and gangs, Caribbean gender and masculinity is intrinsically linked with complex forms of violence. These violences have produced both outlaw and revolutionary masculinity.

Revolutionary masculinity aims to liberate oneself and others while actualizing anti-capitalist and anti-state ideologies. Outlaw masculinity exercises the desire to escape the reaches of the state in pursuit of one's desires, whether for money or freedom. It can involve the harm of other oppressed individuals, outlaws, or revolutionaries.

■ ■ ■

Outlaw masculinity can be traced as far back as 1960s Jamaica, which underwent immense social and political change after the island gained its independence from Britain in 1962. In the late 1950s and early 1960s, it was less common for the gangs that existed in Jamaica to fight each other. This was because one of the reasons that gangs formed was to oppose colonial police civilizing poor urban youth through violence, control, and stigmatization. Violence enacted by impoverished men, like Whoppy King, one of the earliest Jamaican gangsters, existed, but was not a cultural staple quite yet. It was the escapades of Rhyging, a gangster in the 1930s and 1940s known for escaping prison and committing several murders, which made him the original "rude boy" and inspiration for the 1972 film, *The Harder They Come.*

Following independence, the population of Kingston rose exponentially as many countryside Jamaicans flocked to the cities. They hoped to find employment, housing, and urban life. Because of the economic death that many in Trench Town and Jamaican ghettos experienced, rude boy culture manifested as many unemployed resorted to scavenging, pimping, stealing, begging, and gambling to get by. The shift from pre-colonial Jamaica to post-independence Jamaica in the late 1960s and 1970s involved the evolution of rude boys becoming hired hands of Jamaica's two most prominent political parties, the Jamaica Labour Party and the People's National Party. Clinton Hutton defines in *Oh Rudie: Jamaican Popular Music and the Narrative of Urban Badness in the Making of Postcolonial Society* how the state's approval of rude boy behavior cemented them in Jamaican society.

In pre- and post-colonial Jamaica, many of the impoverished men, who became rude boys, created outlaw masculinity. While rude boys were cementing themselves into the national zeitgeist, other configurations of masculinity existed as well. Rastafarians faced consistent repression on the island, being subjected to police raids in their communities, like Kingston's Back O'Wall, which was bulldozed, made into low-income housing, and labeled Tivoli Gardens in the mid 1960s. Even in the newly liberated Jamaica, Rastafarians still faced repression, continued to build a way of life that resisted Babylon, and aided in the less violent expression of manhood.

■ ■ ■

It was this Jamaica of gangs and political and gendered turmoil that my mother and her siblings were born into. My mother often laughed when she talked about running from cows with her sisters on their way home from church or the occasional Rasta service that she went to. She and her siblings learned to raise and slaughter chickens for sale.

"Sometimes while playing in the backyard or in the bush," my mother sometimes exclaimed, "we'd find chains and tools that we later realized were a part of plantation slavery."

The ghosts or the remnants of Jamaica's colonial past were literally the ground that the poor of the island walked upon, left to those who stumbled upon them or had the curiosity to scavenge for them. With few economic opportunities, many of my uncles began to explore the rude boy culture and started to wear sharp clothes, gold chains, and brim hats. They formed bands, tried to play for tourists, and explored Rastafarianism. Derrick was best friends with a slick-looking boy in the neighborhood, Prince, that caught my mother's eye. Maybe she first noticed him playing football in the yard barefoot, his shoulders narrow and skin tanned, sweaty in the sun. Prince wore spectacular prints and acquired the nickname Jazz. My mother was smitten with him and glued their school photos together when she was thirteen years old. He would become my father. In his photo, he wore a striped shirt and a short afro, and stared back at the camera with a morose expression. A portrait of my mother and Prince in the late 1980s rests in my grandmother's basement. His dark eyes probed the onlooker to challenge the lion holding on to his lover. Seven years after the portrait, he died violently; my father, strange fruit, not hanging from a poplar tree, but flung onto the roadside of America. For years, I kept a copy of his death certificate that I'd stumbled upon in the attic of our house. His bruised skin, broken bones, scraped knuckles, and a bullet wound to the back of the head were more than just injuries. They were the life-giving and death-baring details of a ghost.

My mother was born two years after independence and in the same year as the release of Bob Marley and the Wailers' first single, "Simmer Down." It addressed rude boy culture, and was released in hopes of curbing the violence on the island. This was also the same year that nineteen-year-old Bob Marley married a devout Rastafarian woman, Rita Anderson.

In 1972, Michael Manley became prime minister of Jamaica and flagged the United States' attention with his support of Fidel Castro in Communist Cuba. By 1976, political tensions between Manley's Jamaica Labour Party and the People's National Party increased when both parties began to hire gangs composed of rude boys to control electoral territory and harm other political party members. All the while, Marley rose in fame and political significance as he toured the world with the Wailers.

Of Marley's music, Mikal Gilmore wrote in *Rolling Stone* in 2005, "Marley wasn't singing about how peace could come easily to the World but rather how hell on Earth comes too easily to too many. His songs were his memories; he had lived with the wretched, he had seen the downpressers and those whom they pressed down."

Despite his significance, Marley was still a thorn in the elite's side, a "no angel" to someone. Many Jamaicans thought Bob Marley aligned with the island's prime minister after Michael Manley conveniently changed the date of the next election to be close to his concert. Just days before his intended performance at the 1976 "Smile Jamaica" concert, a group of gunmen bombarded Marley's home with bullets before fleeing in the direction of Tivoli Gardens, which was known to be a People's National Party territory.

Jamaican media, much like Marley's music, provides a visual language to the claustrophobia and violence of masculinity marred by Babylon. The films *Shottas* and *Soon Mus Come* all depict Jamaican men exercising outlaw masculinity (or some form of bad boy culture). These men struggle to conceptualize and attain what they feel is important in life. These films, although willing to visualize this conflict through violence or gang warfare, seldom imagine an alternative to outlaw masculinity—a healthier, revolutionary masculinity capable of defeating Babylon personally or systemically.

The 2011 film *Better Mus Come* follows Ricky, a community leader and single father who has lost the mother of his child to gang violence in 1970s Kingston. Throughout the film, Ricky's friends constantly pressure him to lead their friend crew toward earning money to support their families. This dually challenges his masculinity as a leader and "breadwinner," a role that men are often inscribed to embody. The group's desire for economic power and mobility leads them to protecting local politicians in exchange for money, which becomes increasingly complicated for Ricky once he becomes infatuated with a woman that lives in a rival gang's territory.

Rastas are present in *Better Mus Come* to remind Ricky that his path for respect and economic stability through his outlaw lifestyle within Babylon may lead to his demise. A Rasta Elder advises, "You have to correct yourself. You have to know yourself, now, and if you see yourself as a murderer, then go and murder. If righteousness is your calling, then become righteous. But you cannot fight the 'righteous battle' with 'weapons of war.' Or else you've joined 'the army of destruction.'"

In the climax, Ricky runs headfirst toward Babylon's lure and is murdered by its agents, the Jamaican government, during the Green Bay Massacre, which actually occurred in 1978. Even in death, Ricky leaves the burden of raising his child on his lover when he forces her to flee with his son in the night, a further manifestation of the gendered politics of an island filled with slain men and single mothers left to care for the children left behind.

In Rasta Elder's warning is that core belief there is a spiritual awakening in the simpleness of life away from Babylon's influences and evils. When we resist Babylon, death is not something to fear, but rather, a probability we should accept sooner than later. In *The Fire Next Time*, James Baldwin knowingly wrote, "Perhaps the whole root of our trouble, the human trouble, is that we will sacrifice all the beauty of our lives, will imprison ourselves in totems, taboos, crosses, blood sacrifices, steeples, mosques, races, armies, flags, nations, in order to deny the fact of death, which is the only fact we have."

bell hooks described the process, "Asked to give up the true self in order to realize the patriarchal ideal, boys learn self-betrayal early and are rewarded for these acts of soul murder." These sentiments let me know that Black men are both afraid to die and, due to the confines of manhood, often have parts of them die sooner rather than later. Suffering, whether received or caused, becomes a qualification for being a man.

Few Jamaican films exhibit the treacherous consequences of outlaw masculinity more than the 2002 film *Shottas.*

Children of the rude boy–culture era, childhood best friends Biggs and Wayne grow up in the ghettos of 1970s Kingston, then they become outlaw adults in 1990s Jamaica and Miami. In the opening scenes, the boys play cops and robbers, witness a real murder in their neighborhood, and then almost effortlessly rob a local deliveryman to make money that they'll use to get visas for the US. In the essay "(De)Constructing Patriarchal Masculinities in Cess Silvera's *Shottas*," Craig A. Smith elaborates how the quick jump from witnessing murder to committing violent acts cements the male characters in a continual process of "a silent acceptance of violence and trauma as rites of passage for these Black boys into manhood."

By the film's end, Biggs, who is ironically portrayed by Ky-Mani Marley (one of Bob Marley's sons) becomes tired of this lifestyle, suggests to his friends that they move to California to live a more peaceful life. This plan is cut short when an enemy gang shoots up their Miami house and kills Wayne. After anonymously leaving his friend, Mad Max, at the hospital, Biggs avenges Wayne by killing Teddy, the leader of the rival gang, and then flees Miami alone. This desperation for not just the necessities of life but also luxury through a process of brutality is at the center of so many Jamaican films. No matter how vividly the gangster begins to reassess his ways, he cannot fully escape his past.

Biggs's isolation at the film's end shows that outlaw masculinity, more often than not, results in a violent end or loss after we've spent a lifetime denying our truest selves in "soul murder."

"Although they cleaned their lives up," my mother said after the murder of her brothers, "their pasts still followed them."

My mother was right. Babylon leaves its mark and demands its consequences whether you live within it as a law-abiding citizen, or outside of it as an outlaw or revolutionary. Many of the men in my family were raised in the Jamaica of *Better Mus Come* and *Shottas*, forced to navigate the poverty and find ways to use their gender as a way to attain wealth, women, or power. Like the 1980 film *Babylon*, they were forced to reckon with the evils and racism of Babylon in another land.

My mother arrived in the US on the heels of Black families protesting for equal and fair education in the city of Cleveland. The protests culminated partially in the implementation of desegregation busing. She was sent to a predominately white school for her first year of American high school and in the years since alluded to the her white classmates making fun of her patois and her choosing not to attend prom. Imagine her and her siblings, ambling to school together against the stark white of an Ohio winter.

Babylon creates poverty, forces poor people to define themselves through this degradation, and for those that resist, they can meet an untimely end or be displaced. Like many of the women in Jamaican cinema, the women in my family have often been forced to make peace with Babylon and raise children within it. They've tried to teach their sons to be better, more respectable versions of the men that they grew up with.

■ ■ ■

When we were whipped as children by family members, it was partially to beat strength into us and prepare us for the world.

My brother or I were made to grab a belt. One that was not too small or not too large. The crack of the leather came down hard and fast as the interrogation ensued. You cannot move or piss yourself or flinch or, worst of all, jerk your hands away. That earned you a stern gaze. Then the family member would say, "Now you get two more."

To be Black is to weather pain. To use some of the same devices used against us in the plantation fields. Our families must break some part of us to make us less breakable when the world, hungry for Black flesh, tries to break us too. Love can become a submission or mean being willing to feel pain; from the little boy thrashing in the water as his uncle shoots him into the air for a just a moment to the bullet blasting through the back of a skull. The world will break you to make a man out of a boy. The world will try to break you because it can. Because it has to. When the young are not guided in how to make sense of these pasts of violence, they are forced to navigate it on their own. These men, who were boys not taught to reckon with violence, become silences and serve as a psychic tool, a reminder of a world left behind.

With me, maybe my mother had and hadn't broken the cycle. Two truths can exist at once. Your body can be the vehicle that someone else can enter this world through and, even as they stare you in the face, you may still not understand them. Children and parents become strangers to each other. The truths that usually matter the most are the ones that we are willing to face. With me, my mother had broken the cycle with her studious child turned wayward adult.

In her most sentimental moments during my childhood, my mother told me that I was the child that "taught her to love." On nights when she neglected to let me sleep in her bed, I'd lay on a blanket on the floor in front of her bedroom window. As a child in preschool, when my teachers had me close my eyes and pretend to shoot off to space, I sometimes thought about my mother's beauty. She remarked how my love for her when I was a young child sometimes challenged her.

On a winter night when I was fifteen, my mother shook me awake and instructed me to go to the kitchen and listen for any noises in the basement. I, annoyed by the late-night wake-up call and my sense of certainty that we didn't have a burglar in our basement, reluctantly went downstairs to check. When I returned still visibly annoyed, my mother's mood shifted from concerned to enraged. She stared me down in the kitchen, then before I could answer her question about my mood, her hand cracked across my face.

When I wouldn't give her the answer that she wanted, she jerked her body to move toward me again. I tensed, then shoved her away. Something heavy filled her and built a wall between us. She looked at me and said, "You're gonna grow up to be a woman beater, just like your dad. I hope you go to prison, just like he did, and men have their way with you."

When my mother said this, she looked through me darkly and toward a memory. At the time, I thought of how she, like many Black mothers, could say, "If you get mad about me whooping your ass and try to call the police, you'll be dead before they get here," with the same ferocity as when she said, "I'll kill a man before he hits me." Sometimes she would avoid my gaze and add an "again" to the end of the latter phrase. Our love was twisted, but some part of me realized that, for my mother,

I would never be untangled from my father, even if I thought her helping me understand him could help her distinguish him from me.

Because of Babylon, my mother and her family grew up poor, ate whatever they could, and tried to make a life in America plausible. The violence and corruption that kept the poor poor pushed men, like my biological father, to sell drugs, find new names, and live in the underbelly of America when they could. The underbelly of America was profitable for drug dealing and welcomed many men with destructive ways.

■ ■ ■

On a January day in 1995, my father traveled to Rainbow Babies Hospital near downtown Cleveland. As a premature infant, I went through a procession of medical procedures to remove hernias, repair my collapsed lung, make way for feeding tubes, blood transfusions, and weeks hooked up on an oxygen machine. My mother was diligently working to pay the bills and flinched every time the phone rang at her job.

"I feared the worst," she said of the hospital phone calls.

My mother recalls my father looking gaunt and distant in the way that people sometimes notice when they've seen someone for the last time. It was midday in January 1995. Doctors, patients, visitors, and ringing phones buzzed around them.

"The doctors need your blood for a transfusion for him," my mother said. "I want you to be a part of his life, but you have to stop this foolishness. It can't be around him."

Weeks later, my mother, thinned down by the stress of her sickly second child and a recently murdered ex-boyfriend, traveled to Jamaica. My father's funeral was in the church that my grandmother took us to as children on Sundays, us trailing behind her like tired ducklings. The flowers in front of his casket spelled out his nickname, Jazzbo. When I search for the truth of my father, that image of us as children sweating and laboring toward someone else's goal comes to mind. Sometimes the goal, the destination is facing death.

Was I the child trailing behind my grandmother, who symbolized the truth? Or was I my grandmother, forever stuck with some mutilation of her son and the secondary truth that he produced?

I daydreamed about my father's funeral when I found photos of it. In my mind as a child and now, the church is filled and there are so many faces, voices, people, and stories that I do not recognize. One woman arrives with a flask of rum in her purse, muttering under her breath about him, and a man came with a gun in his inside jacket pocket and a Bible in one hand.

My mother arrives. It's hot for a February day, too hot for any day. Far away are the stories of my father's jam band—Derrick trailing behind them with a bag of clothes, Senel with the drums, and my father, Prince, with a guitar—on some downtown strip bobbing to the music and grinning in the sunlight. All old friends.

This space in time enthralls and terrifies me because I want to avoid seeing him this way, the only way I could see him outside of my mind. He is dead. More dead than alive because of all the pain and loss and brutality that he produced. More dead than alive because of what his life stirred those around him, how it had terrified them, and how that, in turn, vanished him even more.

And if that could happen to him, what would it take for it to happen to me?

Cleveland, Ohio, United States, 2010

It was late May in 2010. I would turn sixteen years old in a few weeks. For the last twelve hours, I kept wondering if I should arrive back to this parking lot, if my life was over, and if I dared to save myself from what might come.

"Hey, Ma," I said shyly in the passenger seat of my mother's car.

My mother gripped the steering wheel of her Toyota truck with thin fingers and an ashen look on her face. I could tell from the redness of her eyes and nose that she had been crying. When angry, my mother could shift from explosive lioness to a feline dragging her tail between her legs, prone to bouts of silence. She tucked a bit of black hair behind her ear and pulled out of the parking lot. I watched as the buildings, homes, and stores shifted from the familiar route to the east side of Cleveland where we lived to something else. We neared Luke Easter Park. In the darkness, I could make out the shape of Zelma Watson George Skating Rink.

I went to the rink in the summers as a kid for birthday parties to eat pizza in the booths and pleaded with my mother to give me more quarters so that I could try to win prizes in the claw machine. My outings to the rink stopped when a third-grade classmate asked me out on a date, then failed to show up at the skating rink. I circled the middle of the rink for close to an hour, my head dizzying with each rotation as my mother watched. In my young life, I had never felt such an off-balance feeling fill my entire body until that parking lot at sixteen.

At Cedar Point Amusement Park earlier that day, my friends and I felt the sun on our brown limbs. We ate cotton candy, drank soda, and let the metal rides whip us around, force us into each other, and make us scream. My friends grabbed me with relief. I latched onto them in terror, all while imagining the dozens of ways my life was about to implode. Gone was the boy hoping that his words could stay hidden. Childhood, for a burgeoning writer, meant that I had to hold these moments in my palm with feral intensity. Adulthood meant that I might open my palm and see nothing but air, and finally face the truth. Losing my family was a part of losing childhood. It was also true that we can lose ourselves or others, in parts.

"Where are we . . ." my voice trailed off.

The headlights of my mother's truck illuminated the parking lot. My mother pulled into a spot, then cut the engine. Even though I couldn't see her face, I could feel her eyes on me. Past her figure and out the driver's-side window, another car rested in the spot beside us.

"We're here to talk," she said.

I couldn't get past the "we" and what the darkness in her tone added to the word. The temperature around us rose to the point that I wanted to roll the window down or, better yet, fling the car door open and run. Nearly twenty-four hours before, I was sleeping in my bed when my mother shook me awake. In the delirium between consciousness and sleep, I heard my mother's question in a hushed voice. I responded with "yes" immediately. My answer shifted our entire world together.

We settled in the truck with darkness in walls and layers around us. I wondered, with irony, could this be a scene similar to how my father had died?

In the pit of my belly, even at fifteen, I already knew that being gay meant that I had to be prepared to die. It was the first lesson about the possibility of my own death that I'd learned. Only after this lesson did I learn that being Black meant that I had to be prepared to die too. Locked in the car, heaving for air, fingers around my neck, scratching and pawing and grabbing for the door, trying to get away, trying to flee toward a life that was mine or something away from expectation. What wasn't expected of me was exactly what I discovered myself to be—batty bwoy, faggot, sweet thing, fragile thing, a boy unconcerned with becoming everyone else's definition of a man.

I took a deep breath and exited the truck. The color of champagne shot down from the streetlights all around us. I shivered, wishing that I'd put on my hoodie or taken my bag out of the car to make it easier to run. I tensed as the driver's-side door of the car next to us opened, then closed. The small figure of a dark woman walked around the car, then faced us.

"Tell your aunt what you told me this morning," my mother said.

I began to sweat as I stood in front of the two most important women in my life. Aunt Vick was the last of her siblings to immigrate to the United States in the early 1980s. With six siblings and no money, my aunt stayed behind while her mother went to the US. Aunt Vick looked after her brothers and sisters, my mother included. My grandmother worked to earn visas and send her children to the States.

"It was kind of like she raised us in a way," my mother once said.

It made sense that Aunt Vick would be my mother's confidant. With water, flour, and salt, anyone could make dumplings, but not everyone could cultivate a home. Jamaica and its poverty were hard on my mother and her siblings, but surely in different ways. For Black or Caribbean families, boys are raised to be providers, aggressors, defenders, and silencers of women. My Jamaican family was littered with men who came to the United States, sold drugs, spent time in prison, and were deported. It was also littered with women forced into the background, piled heavy with sacrifices and the responsibilities of caring for the young.

"Why did you keep this secret from us?" my mother asked.

I was suddenly aware of how alone we were. My mother with her arms crossed in front of her and my aunt clutching her purse. Just a year before, I sat in front of my laptop and read through exactly how Matthew Shepard was murdered. The image of his body strung up like a scarecrow was burned into my head so vividly that I covered his murder for a class assignment. Then came the Google searches of the violence against queer people in Jamaica.

Even if I was safe, I was in for a reckoning. It was my hands and my hands only that could guide me home now. I saw no point in holding my tongue anymore. The words, however, came out shakily.

"I couldn't trust you. I didn't trust you," I replied. "What reason did I have to?"

My mother's face contorted and I couldn't decide if the folds of her expression made her ugly or sad. Aunt Vick edged closer to her but didn't extend any physical reassurance. Her gaze shifted between my mother and me. My mother wiped her face, trying to rid herself of the tears as they fell freely.

"But a we grow yuh. We fed yuh. We sent you to school. We—"

"You joked about gay people being killed."

They didn't have a response. Aunt Vick, someone usually not so nervous, looked like a hostage negotiator. I could handle my secret being outed to someone that looked at me with a pensive gaze. What I couldn't handle was what this situation could become if I didn't steer it in the right direction.

"I think what Prince a try fi say is that he muss been afraid fi tell you, you know? He's a smart bwoy."

My mother's laser vision returned. She unfolded her arms and seemed as if she was about to stomp.

"You're fifteen years old. You barely live yuh life yet and now you're under all these influences. You're going to change your mind."

"If there was any influence that I was under," I replied, "it was all the jokes about gay people. All the snickering when you passed them in stores. Changing the channel when you saw them on TV. You don't get to choose whether what you say hurts people."

My mother raised her hand abruptly and opened her mouth to make another point. Aunt Vick shot her a glance that was affirming, yet stern.

Part of me loved and part of me hated that Aunt Vick was even there. Or maybe my anger was more about the fact that she only worked as a light buffer to my mother's anger and assumption. I did not want an ally that batted away my humiliation with soft words. That sort of ally meant that the conflict I produced mattered more than how the conflict harmed me or what it stole. It meant being buried alive by good intentions with tape over my mouth.

I had to speak up next. "I've spent years thinking and trying to change it. Being unhappy didn't make sense anymore."

My mother crossed her arms and shook her head.

"It just doesn't make sense. You let yuh friends, these girls, make you think that acting this way is okay. Yuh shud worry about school, getting good grades, and being ready for college. Wah you waan fi duh?"

I felt the pressure rush to my eyes. We all stood in silence. I crossed my arms and brought them closer to my body as I shivered again. The thought washed over me. How did I get here? Why was this happening to me?

I stared back at my mother, and there it was, the look that had crossed her face so distinctly in the early-morning hours as we sat in our basement and talked—disgust. Then she said it again, "This ain't how we raise you."

"Maybe that's a good thing."

I clenched my teeth, inhaled deep, and exhaled deeper. I knew that if I started crying, then I wouldn't stop. What mattered most in the moment was that I didn't show weakness, or better yet, that I didn't show regret.

"Look, I just wanna go home. I'm tired," I said. "I—"

"We have to talk about this," my mother interjected.

I shook my head and leaned my back against her Toyota truck. The sudden surge of regret made me dizzy. I wished that I hadn't kept that journal. I wished that she hadn't scoured my room, found it, and read my life's most pressing secret. She said she'd done it because she was worried about how rocky our relationship had become. I knew that was a lie. You don't search for the truth about someone you love, only to try to tuck it away when it doesn't fit into your worldview. Shouldn't love be about wanting to face the darkness together, not alone?

There should be no turning back from the truth when your son will spend the rest of his life loving a man, fucking a man, marrying a man, and hoping the man treats him right. And if you did turn away, you were simply omitting a truth that has already been written and swallowed and was living inside of me.

In my years of self-questioning, I quickly realized one of my largest fears about life as a gay man in a disapproving family—how part of all of my life's best moments would always be reserved for coping with familial rejection. The worst of all—walking toward my husband on my wedding day, empty-handed of a mother, perpetually waiting for her to swallow her pride. Or to protect me from the world in the way that I needed to be protected. My future was a graveyard in its infancy. I tried to speak again, but this time I accepted that my voice shook.

"When I was ten years old, I heard Daddy say that if he had a gay son, he would kill him. Do you even remember that?"

They both froze and refused to stare at each other; they only stared at only me.

"But that wasn't about you," my mother said.

It seemed like a line from some bad Hallmark movie. Only it was something that my mother was actually saying to me. I had to laugh. Did she want a private show of my years of battling myself? Did anyone ever talk gleefully about killing gay people and not really wanting to do it if given the chance?

"You wouldn't say that if someone hurt me because of it one day."

It was an ironic thing for me to say. I was already standing in a sea of hurt and trying to tread my way back to the shore. This night was my reckoning. My feet leaving one room and moving to the other.

We got back into the car. My mother drove us home in silence. I couldn't shake the thought that maybe I was already dead to my mother. That night I was unable to sleep knowing she was in the next room. It wasn't only that I was being rejected. It was also that I didn't completely understand why. Or how it happened in this way. I couldn't have known when I scribbled in journals and believed that words would save me and not haunt me, that those words would become my undoing with her too.

I'd spent months with my journal. Slowly, but surely I inched toward the truth about myself to myself. I also inched toward not being afraid to write it down and see it permanent in ink. The act of my body choosing to make the admission physical and not simply assuming it because my peers did was a revelation. This realization began a little death. I was just uncertain who was the murderer of spirit and who was the victim.

I lay in bed and thought of her face as she stared back at me, love buried deep under a layer of disgust. I had surely seen it before when I was eleven years old. My mother and I were in the living room. She looked at me, her face etched with disgust and she asked, "Are you gay?"

I was less sure of myself then. I was also drowning in a life that I didn't have the courage to step into yet and in a sea of future betrayals. I wrinkled my nose, shook my head, and whispered "no." I don't know what my life would be like now if she had knelt down, grabbed my face with both hands, and said with the force of Mama Wati, "God loves you and he loves me too. I can save you from drowning." The thought of where my life would be if that had happened is both stirring and terrifying. That memory, unlived, could have had the impact of the Big Bang, a single shift that breaks the cycle and creates something new.

This is the truth that I tried to get across to my mother in that parking lot, to my brother when he found me in the basement during my freshman year of college when he told me to "grow up." We cannot love people based on the illusions that we've built around them. We have to engage with their reality and be willing to face it with them. This action requires courage and a dismantling. It is love, like a fire, that aims to consume everything before it and threatens to liberate more the next time.

Even then in my sickness as a premature infant in the intensive care unit, she watched, waited, and prayed for me to grow more capable and strong. What had changed between then and now as an outed teenager?

Shortly after that night my mother enrolled me in therapy. In our first session, my mother was invited to talk to the therapist with me. I looked the therapist squarely in the face, fidgeted in my seat, and asked, "I just need to know that I'm safe. How would you define mental and physical abuse?"

The therapist was a young white woman with a warm demeanor. Her brown hair touched her ears. She looked between my mother and me in the narrow office and cleared her throat before explaining the difference between the two.

"Are you experiencing either of those things?"

I looked at my mother for a defying moment and shook my head "no" while feeling the fight leave me. Even in my righteous defiance, I still had a sense that my anger went beyond the current situation. My betrayal was tinged with the fact that it hurt to know that my mother, a Black woman in a race that often admonished therapy, thought that I was deviant enough to necessitate help that she couldn't give me. Though it felt like I was dead to my mother, it also felt like a part of me was dying too. I was irritable, seemingly unloved, and being prodded by hands larger than mine. My fighting spirit couldn't win every battle. So therapy was my compromise.

Therapy unexpectedly became a haven, a place where an adult could tell me that it wasn't unreasonable to want parents that could accept your sexuality. It also became a place that I could be challenged. In one of my solo sessions with the therapist, I vented about how much I despised my parents for how much they'd subconsciously made me feel like I should hate myself.

My therapist stared back and said, "You do realize there's going to be a day when you don't live with them, a day when you'll have to decide to let go of this anger. You can't choose your parents. You choose how you react to them."

Her honesty softened me, forced me to think toward a future where I wouldn't be living at home. It didn't erase the harder parts of coming out, when I felt like a caged animal trying to squeeze myself through the bars to get to sunlight.

"And what if it's always like this?"

I wanted to fold inside of myself on the blue couch. I hated the fact that I was already crying. The words kept flying out of my mouth.

"This week she yanked me out of the house and walked me down the street to just ask, 'Why do you want to be a faggot?'"

My therapist handed me a tissue and I blew my nose. We sat in silence for a few moments. In therapy, there always seemed to be a moment when the patient goes too deep too quickly. Then the therapist's reaction is rehearsed shock or waiting for the patient to say more.

"Why have a kid that you can't even love in the way that they need to be loved? Why be afraid of something you brought into the world?"

My therapist's face shifted under the heat of my question, then became determined on the thought that crossed her mind. She sighed and set aside her clipboard.

"You know more than most people that there are many different kinds of love with all sorts of horrible things mixed in."

I wanted to turn away from her, yell, and say that she was excusing my mother or that I didn't need more vague platitudes tossed my way like a bone. But my mind was trapped on the words that she chose to use. My mother had said horrible things. The more I thought of what she said and of my mother's righteousness, the more I respected the twisted, underlying meaning of my therapist's words. For some, love meant helping someone get free. For others, love meant falling in line or doing the right thing. Even the love that had coaxed me into the world was marred with horrible things.

I couldn't recall when my mother told me the story of my birth for the first time, only that it felt less like a birth story and more like a ghost (or duppy) story, something to gaze back on, but an event one won't willingly relive. But the story goes like this.

With her belly plump, she calls my father to give a pregnancy update, maybe also to reprimand him for his most recent life mishandling. Her sister just left for the store in her rickety black car on that June day. The tree in the backyard is fertile, green, alive.

Instead of my father's almost baritone voice aged by prison, the yard, and the posturing, a softer voice answers.

"I'm sorry," a woman's voice says to my mother. "Who is this?"

My mother's face becomes a valley of lines as she tries to distinguish who the woman who answered her boyfriend's phone is. Her eyes widen as the realization settles in. There is a long pause. Blood rushes everywhere and nowhere as my mother stands. People told her that this might happen. That man is a dog. He is incapable of love. Didn't he hurt you before? Jamaican bwoys a no good fi noting but di devil. He look fi di devil. Her palms are sweating and the voice on the other end of the phone grows louder, louder, morphing into a duppy. The voice expects my mother to scream back, to reach deep into her throat, and pull out the woman that would fight for her love.

"Me wid him now," the beguiling voice says.

There is a kick, a scream, and panic. Everything around my mother turns into a washing machine, a tsunami, an audience of television cameras and mouths laughing, twisted and cracked from the heat. The phone falls from her hand and suddenly the thing inside of her feels much less like a thing. It is moving. Her lower half heats up and the tsunami has brought a mountain of wet down beneath her.

The next days are spent in rain or storm or with beautiful skies as the doctor in the hospital is aware that this thing, no, wait, this baby inside of her is ready for screaming life.

It's too soon. It's too soon. God damn this man. God damn him and everything that he came with. If this is what you get for love, then love for men is just a warm body in sweaty sheets.

Sometimes the positioning of her body makes her want to scream. Not because it hurts, but because things dressed up as love and deliverance can so easily contort the body, make waste of the body, shift the almost body inside of the body.

The doctors cannot wait any longer. The duppy moves along the ceiling, lips shut with thick, purple stitches. She is scared as they wheel her through rooms. In the last room, it happens. The almost body leaves the full body. My mother waits for the scream that never comes. The duppy never swoops down to claim the malignant thing, just floats in the ceiling's corner.

There is still no scream. The parade of doctors slows down. The white man now floats over my mother's head and breathes.

"Do you want us to do everything to save this baby?"

The duppy's long, reddened fingers reach for its mouth and start to pull apart the stitches. Before it can pop all of them open, my mother stares up at the white man. The duppy flies away and latches itself to its list of men; a string, a black hole crosses the distance from this quiet body surrounded by doctors to a father. The timer is set. The duppy chuckles, far away.

My mother responds. Her voice is strong.

"Do everything you can."

My first few months are a procession of infant beds that looked like cages, blood transfusions, surgeries to inflate my lungs, and hernias. From the start, I have to be prepared to die if I really wanted to live. My mother and Aunt Vick stare at my frail body in the NICU in the February after my birth. My mother, walking through a fog as she thought of the horror of it, might mutter, "Thrown out of a car. Can you imagine?"

Aunt Vick looks at my mother and says the only thing she could. "Some people have to die so other people can live."

This baby is quiet. Its skin is no longer almost clear to the point that its organs are visible. After all, babies born too ready for the world need mothers to help thicken their skin. Some babies are born riding along rainbows and some tread the darkness with the duppy of death watching. I am born to both.

Cleveland, Ohio, United States,
and Montego Bay, Jamaica, 1999–2000

I was four years old when the same dream haunted me every night for nearly a year. In every dream, the season changed. Sometimes snow covered the tree swing in the backyard of the red-and-white house that my mother, brother, and I lived in. In another season, dying autumn leaves covered the front yard. In the dream, we always sat in the bedroom that my brother and I shared. I ripped off the gift wrap of a present as I sat next to my mother, who was slender and dressed in a white turtleneck. My brother squealed while peeling open a box of sneakers. My mother cackled and clapped at his excitement.

"Mommy, I forgot my phone in your room," I said.

"Alright," my mother said as she patted my back. "Get it and come back."

I held Henry, a teddy bear, tight in my arms as I jumped down from the bed. Aside from Henry, my toy phone was my next favorite toy. I walked out into the short hallway and then stopped just before entering my mother's doorway. A woman dressed in all white with ashen skin floated there. Her arms hung at her sides. Her expression, both omnipotent and kind, unnerved me. She glowed as I stood trapped in her gaze with my palms sweating. The dream always moved through my body like a lightning rod. I'd awaken with the air hanging around me in my dark room. Under the covers, I'd pull Henry closer and called my brother's name. He'd be tangled, sleeping, and snoring.

It would be months before the dream took on a new meaning, the first of many things to pitch itself upward and cast a shadow over my life. Just another of the many mysteries to come. No matter how many times I awakened, wiped my eyes, and tried to relay the details of the dream to my mother or brother, their response was always the same. I was always the child with the overactive imagination that liked books.

There were times when I attempted to ask my mother what the meaning of the dream was, but I don't recall her occasional replies resonating with me. My mother worked or paid bills or, if she had the time, helped us do our homework. My older brother, on the other hand, listened as I recalled the dream.

"Maybe she's there to tell you how much of a crybaby you are," he replied while shading in a coloring book as he sat on his bed.

Even at a young age, I sometimes sensed that things were being felt and experienced around me. Adults had a world of their own and sometimes children got glimpses of it. One day, my mother showed me a photograph and told me that I was going on a trip soon.

"Here he is," my mother said as she placed the photo in my hand. "Your father."

The camera was pointed downward at a man who sat with his legs crossed. He was wearing gray pleated pants, a white tank top, and sunglasses as he sat next to a bed. The photo was maybe snapped in the middle of him saying something. He seemed suave, a characteristic that was later corroborated when I learned to read his writing on the back of the photo, "How you like me now? Fresh is the word." The flash shone at the light-brown skin of his forehead. I wondered who he was talking to and why I had never met him. I also wondered if meeting someone through a photograph even made sense. Was it the same as sticking your hand out to meet a ghost?

"Always remember how important family is. Friends will come and go, but blood is thicker than anything else," my mother said. "That's why this trip is so important."

She smiled, kissed me on the forehead, and then left the room. I sat holding the photo and imagined myself shaking my father's hand. I began the lifelong journey of piecing him together in my mind.

■ ■ ■

My mother arrived in Cleveland, Ohio, in the early 1980s when the city was being morphed by years of political unrest. Gone was the one-room house for her and her six siblings, running from cows after church on Sundays, the bun and cheese at the bakery down the street from Albion Prep, and the laughter of the neighborhood children when the street gutters filled with rainwater to swim in. In the brush behind their house, my mother and her siblings played. The boys pretended to be cowboys with weapons made of sticks and stones. The girls played with DIY dolls.

Cleveland hosted the famed "Ballot or the Bullet" speech by Malcolm X and had white mobs attacking Black parents in Little Italy in defense of school segregation in 1964. The city had the nation's first Black mayor in 1967 and a Black downtown that was stolen from its people in 1983. My mother entered the American schooling system during a period of violent transition in the early 1980s as a part of desegregation busing. In newspaper articles, Cleveland parents talked about their children being made to do gym class in the hallways or having only one chance a day to use the restroom.

The grief from school and a whole new culture was surely worth it compared to the chaos in the Jamaica that they'd left—an economy going downward due to exploitative aid from other countries, rude boys joining gangs, talk of government corruption, a national state of emergency, and even an attempted assassination on Bob Marley at his home. So my mother took what America offered, like many other women in my family, got her high school diploma, and found work.

When she had a break on nights and weekends from being a cosmetologist, she frequented Dailey's, a Caribbean market and bar on East 116th Street. Past the aisles of plantain chips, champagne sodas, and beef patties, she could find a back room. Bodies swayed and sweated. People passed around bottles of Red Stripe beer and walked through marijuana haze. Life could not just be about work. It could also be about dance, seeing friends, and finding love.

The men in my family tended to find murkier paths. In 1987, two of my mother's brothers, Senel and Derrick, were arrested on drug charges and sentenced to two years in prison.

Their subsequent deportations meant leaving wives, children, lovers, and family in the United States.

What mattered more than the illusions of the American Dream were the ways that race, gender, and birthplace shaped the reality of America for my family. My grandmother working as a cleaning woman for white families in the 1970s. The racism of my mother's white classmates. And eventually, the hold that the War on Drugs would have on the many men of my family. Then the struggles to untangle homophobia from my family's culture, police violence, and global anti-Blackness in my own lifetime.

At the dawn of a new decade, the 1990s, my mother's body started to change. A doctor's test confirmed her suspicion. Around the time that my brother's fetus began detecting sound and grew to eight inches, twenty-six-year-old Rodney King would be apprehended after trying to flee police. Officers slammed batons against his ankles, wrists, elbows, and knees. He was tasered twice. He suffered eleven skull fractures, broken bones, and brain damage. Another Black body proven to be prey for America.

Upon hearing news of King's beating, my mother, wrapped in her work and filled with her strength, might have thought, "What horrible things does America have in store for my child?"

She gave birth to my brother in 1991. After the hardness of labor and calamity of his birth, she held her first son in her arms. His pale skin, soft hair, and silken magic ruptured awe. Her brothers wheeled her out of the hospital. She stared up at the sky in the cool Cleveland afternoon. Another thought engrossed her mind. This time it was, "How do I do this? How do I raise another human being?"

No answers came. My brother stirred in her refuge, and like all Black mothers do, my mother moved forward. My mother found a way.

■■■

The airport tarmac was hot, black, and wide. Almost five years old in early summer of 1999, I stood in jean shorts and a yellow tank top. My skin was melting from the slather of Vaseline my mother rubbed on me earlier. Now my whole body felt like it was overheating. Around us, the white tourists walked, their skin coated with sunscreen and shaded under bucket hats. Other people walked by with dark sable skin while wearing mesh tops and shorts or dresses.

"You're going to get on the plane and your auntie is going to pick you up when you get there," my mother said as she straightened my shirt.

My mother glowed in the Miami daylight as she handed me over to the flight attendant for my final connecting flight to Jamaica. My mother wore jeans, black boots, and a shimmery gray top. A gold crucifix necklace dangled around her slender neck. Her bracelets made music as she used her spit to wipe my face.

"You coming to see me though, right?" I asked.

She smiled, tried to stop her lips from shaking, and hugged me again.

"You'll be back before you even know it. Just remember what I said. Brush yuh teeth every night. Listen to your auntie and grandmother. Don't give them no trouble and be nice to your sister, Princess, when you meet her. Be good."

The flight attendant took my hand and nodded reassuringly in my mother's direction. As we walked away, I decided I wouldn't turn back to look at my mother. I didn't want to see her cry. So I stared up at the flight attendant instead. She was tall and dark, and smiled at me. We climbed the narrow steps to the small plane. Everything about the machine was loud, shiny, and beautiful.

"Have you ever been on a plane before?" the flight attendant asked as she buckled me in. I wondered what she used to brush her teeth because they were so white.

"I seen them on TV sometimes, but I didn't know I'd be on one of them today. Do you know why my mom isn't coming with me?"

The flight attendant thought for a moment as she put my backpack under my seat.

"Your mommy wants you to see your family, but she has to work to make money for you. What does your mommy do for work? She's very pretty."

"I know she's pretty," I said with a smirk. "She fixes people's hair."

A few minutes later, the plane's engines got louder. A weird feeling moved through my stomach. Suddenly, I didn't like looking out the window at the tarmac so much. The flight attendant came over again to give me apple juice and cookies. I tore open the cookie package carefully and tried not to mess up the hippo's face on it. I liked that the cream inside of the cookies were strawberry flavored. I tried to not eat all of them right away.

■■■

The heat in Jamaica was what I noticed first. Different from the summer heat of Ohio, Jamaica was humid no matter how many windows you opened and how much breeze you hoped for. A June day could have you screaming if you jumped onto the tile without flip-flips on while it baked in the sun. When I burned my feet for the first time, I screamed and ran back to the shade as Princess, Tomita, and Kristina laughed.

My grandmother often kept my cousins and me inside when the sun towered above us during midday. When I first arrived, they were most excited to rummage through the bag of toys that my mother had packed for me.

The sisters, Kristina and Tomita, immediately fought over the dolls that my mother bought for the girls to have. Kristina, who was older and stronger, easily grabbed the brunette doll while shoving her sister away. Our grandmother shrieked when she saw Princess and me leafing through the same coloring book while deciding which pictures we'd draw.

"Oh God bless mi fi di chance to see Prince's pickney together," she said while corralling my sister and me together on her front steps. My new sister, Princess, was lean and copper skinned just like the man in the photo that my mother had shown me. I wondered why I looked darker if we were siblings. My grandmother's camera flashed. Princess and I rushed back inside.

That summer, my cousins, my sister, and I spent nearly every moment together. When picking up bag juice from the small shop near the road, Tomita, Princess, and I trailed behind

Kristina like tiny ducks, our little feet jumping into the shade that trees provided along the way. Kristina taught us how to play jacks, how to play Go Fish, and how to not give ourselves away during hide-and-seek. Princess and I giggled too much when we hid in the same place together.

Our playground was my grandmother's large yard filled with plants, stones, dogs, and red ants. We hid among the plants and under beds inside of the house during hide-and-seek. After lunch, I liked to help my grandmother, a warm woman that wore long dresses, feed the pack of dogs that she kept. She piled old rice, meat, and bones into a cast-iron pan before putting it into the dogs' bowls. I loved her dogs even if they weren't very nice.

I soon learned that Sundays were an operation of their own. My grandmother woke us early, set up cold showers for us, put a towel over our shivering bodies, and for the next hour, ironed our clothes, coated our skin with Vaseline, and braided the girls' hair. After she called us, we ate breakfast at the cramped dining room table, still in our underwear. Cornmeal porridge was my favorite. The liquid was thick, warm, and sweet. Princess showed me how it tasted better when she added chunks of hard dough bread. After food, we put on our starch-stiffened clothes and walked under the beating sun.

Sunday school started before noon and was in the back room on the church's second floor. A dozen of us kids sat under the fan yawning, trying not to fall asleep, or pinching each other. The actual church service was even longer than Sunday school. While grandma was screaming and shouting to God, it was Kristina's job to kick us awake when we fell asleep. It wasn't rare for me to jolt awake to people standing up in the rows screaming, waving Bibles around, and begging God to help their family.

"Why do people scream like that?" I asked Tomita as we left the church one day.

She shrugged and scratched at her black pigtails. Her dress was dark purple. I couldn't stop staring at her shiny shoes. It perplexed me how long adults spent on getting girls dressed only to tell them that they crossed their legs wrong in public when people stared at them. Why give girls shiny shoes and pretty outfits, but not the boys?

"I think if you don't show God that you're afraid of him, he punishes you by sending you to burn in hell when you dead. That's what the Sunday school lady said."

I held on to Princess's and Tomita's hands as we walked away from church. I wasn't sure if fearing God made any sense to me. Why would he make us if he wanted us to be afraid? And weren't all people good and bad? Whenever my mother told me about scary things, she also told me it was her job to protect me.

After church, Grandma moved around the kitchen fiercely. Tomita, Princess, and I often followed Kristina as she fulfilled her duty as the cooking assistant because she was the oldest. We peeled open ackee, plucked callaloo, gathered bunches of thyme, and measured out the coconut milk for the rice and beans. At the table, the smell of scotch bonnet peppers, garlic, and spices filled the air. Usually a picky child, I learned to fall in line with my new family by eating whatever was served.

"You love dumpling soh," my grandmother exclaimed. "You always ask fi ten. Yo eyes bigga den yo stomach."

Getting along was more than just eating the food put in front of me. It was realizing when it was important to listen to adults around you and follow their rules, even if you were experiencing a new culture. I also noticed the difference between my clean, white American teeth and my sister's decaying teeth. I learned from how the neighborhood kids scrambled to my grandmother's gate to look at my Game Boy, the envious looks they gave me when I told them my mommy didn't let people other than my family touch my expensive things. A kid from America and a kid in Jamaica could grow up with very different things.

As soon as I landed on the island, the dream of the woman floating in my mother's doorway stopped. One night, my cousins, my sister, and I huddled together while sitting on a bed in an extra room in my grandmother's house. Outside the crickets buzzed and a strong breeze rattled the louver windows. A trail of gray floated up to the ceiling from a mosquito smoke coil in the corner.

"We got one duppy that is one big ole woman and she have big, big breasts," Tomita said gravely as we all stared at each other through the flashlight glow. "If she want chase you and hit you down wit her breasts and breath fiya pon yo, you dead so."

I didn't have Henry to hug since I'd left him in his bed in my room in Ohio, so I clutched the pillow that was against my chest. Grandma's house always made strange creaky noises at night and it didn't help that we watched *Highway to Hell* for the fifth time earlier that day.

"My mommy told me if you married and yo man die, he can come back as a duppy to find you," Princess explained.

That night, Princess and I fell asleep with our arms grasping at each other as we dreamed. At the time, I couldn't place it, but an unspoken bond was building between us. At church, on the street, or with other family members, it was common for us to be fawned over or greeted with teary eyes. To everyone else, we were the living reincarnations of our father, walking around in his likeness and summoning the dead. To each other, we were new friends, if not new family, trying to move through the expectations that every comparison of us to our father surmounted.

About once a week, Princess's mother would come to Grandma's house to check in on her or pick her up for a few days. Her mother was petite with black hair and dark-brown eyes. She called Princess with a stern air and brushed by me quickly. I couldn't tell that my presence summoned a sort of bitterness in Princess's mother. How could I have known that I was also a reincarnation of his beauty and conquests?

■■■

The humid summers of running around the underbelly of my grandma's house gave way to the fall. Home was as far away as my mother's voice on the phone. She reassured me that this trip was important, that my father's side of my family deserved to see me. So important that my auntie sat me down to tell me that I would be starting school soon in Jamaica, not America.

"No school with my brother?" I said, wiping my nose. "I wanted him to sit with me at lunch."

My auntie held my hand and rubbed the skin there. She smiled.

"You'll get to go to school with Tomita. You don't have to be so nervous."

I sat on her couch by the front door and stared outside. The Jamaican sky was turning a distinct champagne with nearly no clouds. Kids laughed and played in the street, only running out of it when cars honked. I thought of how nice it was to play with kids outside here, unlike my neighborhood back home where my mom liked for us to stay inside.

"So I'm staying here," I said.

"Until the end of the school year."

The two-story cement school building was foreboding. Past the thick, gray front and then down the hallway, I passed five classrooms. Each room had long tables with chairs and a massive chalkboard. While studying math or spelling, we were lucky if the ceiling fans were strong enough to relieve us. My uniform of khaki shorts, a cotton button-down shirt, blue tie, and dress shoes wasn't forgiving in the heat.

If the temperatures got too high, I would feel a strange rush through my face and then a wet feeling in my nose before the blood droplets came rushing out. The teacher rushed to me with a roll of toilet paper. I walked through the classroom of snickers as I went to the nurse. Being the American boy was already enough to make me stick out. Now I was also the sissy that got nosebleeds.

"You sweet so in America, you can't even handle a likkle island heat," said a girl with a red scrunchie as I walked by. Laughter bounced off the cement walls.

Tomita was the only one that could really help me with the teasing. At first, I didn't really complain about it. Just tried to keep to myself. Sometimes she found me sitting on a cement ledge in the school's dusty courtyard, crying openly. If kids decided to mess with me, she kicked up a cloud of dust and stuck her tongue out at them. If it came down to it, she insulted them too.

"Why tun neva big up yuhself when them call you Big Head?" she asked me during a recess.

Tomita sucked on bag juice. The liquid ran down her arms as she gulped.

"I don't know," I replied as I handed her the rest of my bun and cheese. But I knew what I couldn't say, which was that I just didn't like being angry or reacting, and that all of the teasing about the way I talked made me feel bad. I heard the adults whispered about how I needed to be a man that stood up for myself. I preferred to blend into the background.

"We can teach you patois," Tomita said. I perked up and nodded because she had only partially read my mind.

Since Princess and I didn't go to the same school, and Tomita and I did, I started to grow closer to Tomita too. Only with her could I vent about my most recent bully or eat candies during recess. She was the only one that looked out for me while all the adults whispered to my mom on the phone about my grades or if I was making friends.

One of the few adults that I felt that I could talk to was Reggie. He lived with our grandmother and was a part of the Jamaican military. Young, limber, and bald, Reggie liked to sit on the front steps of our grandmother's house and polish his shoes on days when the clouds occasionally cut off the sunlight. He popped a CD into his radio and sang along to Toni Braxton while I rubbed old rags with shoe polish, then handed them to him. A man in his twenties, Reggie was wise to me. He seemed responsible because of the way he talked about his military benefits. He kept a poster of Toni Braxton next to his bed and liked to describe all of the dates that he would take her on. From her breasts to her voice to her skin, Reggie's descriptions helped me learn what most people found beautiful about women.

"You're a smart boy. Now you just have to go back to the US and make your momma proud. You know how you'll do that?"

I shrugged and slipped my feet into his army boots. The boots reached halfway up my legs. I liked that he was good at asking questions and listening.

"You get good grades. You grow up, get a job, and help your ma out, just like I'm helping grandma," Reggie explained. "These women are the backbone of our family."

Another cousin, Frank was the opposite of Reggie. He wore white tank tops that sparkled against his even darker skin. He entered our grandma's yard, slamming the gate behind him and running up the front steps with groceries. He greeted all of us loudly, wrapped his arms around Grandma, and gave her a kiss on the cheek. She swooned and fixed her glasses on her nose to look at him more clearly.

"You look ten years younga from di last time mi saw you, Grandma."

Grandma blushed in response.

With us, Frank liked to pick out silly movies and laugh heartily with us as we watched. If he and Reggie ever drank, he pulled me aside from all the other girls and had me sit down with them. The Red Stripe beer sweat when he placed one in my hand. The two men looked at me expectantly.

"Wah gwan?" Frank said. "Men in the States nah drink no beer?"

Frank elbowed Reggie, who tried to cover his trembling lips with his hand. I drank from the tip of the bottle and coughed.

"You gwan learn fi drink and learn fi lick up dem bwoy in your grade. You gwan learn some bad man tings," Frank continued saying.

Even with how much I liked Reggie, I often wondered how he could be so nice to me and still let Frank say things like that when we were around each other. Adults liked telling me how important it was for me to stand up for myself, but I wondered if the world would just be a better place if people stood up for each other or if more people would be like Tomita, brave and willing to speak. It seemed like older men had been given some kind of list of rules. Maybe one day when I was old enough, I would do the right set of things to finally be given these rules. Until then, it was just my job to survive being a good boy.

After all, what was so good about being a bad man?

■ ■ ■

At the time, it was just another normal night. Tomita, Kristina, Princess, and I sat in our cousin's room around a circular table. Kristina threw a bag of plantain chips at Princess from the pile of snacks and shuffled the cards. For a long time, we had a contest to see who could win the most of any games that we played, whether it be racing, tag, marbles, jacks, or hide-and-seek. My throat burned as I drank a pineapple soda.

"We're gonna start with Go Fish, Kristy," Princess exclaimed as her braids bobbed. "You said we could earlier!"

"Well, I think I'm gonna win," Tomita said as she sat straighter in her chair.

I stuck my tongue out at her and Princess laughed. Soon we were deep into the game, sipping at our sodas and gnawing on cheese snacks. No one wanted to leave because the stakes were simply too high. I took a risk during Go Fish and asked for threes.

"No!" exclaimed Princess. She grimaced even after handing over two of her cards.

After an hour of playing, there was a knock at the bedroom door. Frank's figure came looming into the room. He stood there. Stared. Smiled. Then he spoke, "Y'all got a good card game?"

We all nodded. Princess's eyebrows pursed together as she stared at her cards. Frank came closer and gazed over the table, then he nudged Tomita.

"Come on. I want to show you something."

Tomita took his hand and they walked out of the room. We stared as they left. Princess looked up from her cards. She smiled with a few teeth missing, then said, "Do I get her cards?"

No one answered. The room fell into a strange silence and I wondered how long they would be gone.

■ ■ ■

A few days after the game night, I was at the end of another hallway. Only this time, I was awake. The outside sky was dark blue and choked with gray clouds. Earlier I rushed to close all the windows with my grandma and help gather the dogs to the underside of the house where it was drier. Still, the rain blew into the house in bursts from the raging wet outside. My slippers squeaked against parts of the linoleum floor. After using the bathroom, I stepped into the hallway. Two figures were in grandma's room, waving their hands, opening their mouths wide, and shouting. The power was out, so the only time that I could make out their expressions was when lightning flashed. Auntie and Uncle were screaming. They cried, grabbed their coats, and eventually left. In all of my months in Jamaica, I had never seen them so angry.

My mind drifted to the dream in Ohio and I realized the difference between that scene and this one. The scene unfolding in front of me was much worse. Worse because something bad and real had happened. Worse because the storm roaring outside had torn something in my little world apart.

I couldn't remember much of my time in Jamaica after the thunderstorm. My lack of memory said more than anything else. I didn't remember any talks with the adults about what had happened on game night or what everyone had screamed about when the power was out. Going along with family, I learned, also meant just choosing to move forward. So I read for my classes, played with my cousins, and continued going to church. Maybe it was like Grandma often said, "God takes care of the important things."

Eventually the school year ended and my mother told me I was coming back to America. The island wavered in my mind and before my eyes in the stinging summer heat. Home, Henry, and my mother sounded like a nice change.

"It's time," my grandmother said.

She marched Tomita, Kristina, Princess, and me to any empty spot in the yard. We squinted up at her in the midday sun. She handed us each a coconut. I ran my fingers over the rough, stringy skin and held it to my chest.

"You know you gwan grow up and change and get big up so. We gwan watch yuh grow just like one coconut tree."

She dug holes for each of us to put our coconuts in. My sister and I went first. I planted the coconut tree, covered it with red dirt, and stepped away. Princess and I glanced at each other, then up at the sky, dizzied by the thought that something we planted could grow to be so big. The two trees, which were planted here and so far away from my life in America, became a symbol of our similarity and difference. Two plants of the same species being on the same patch of land was not the same as being identical or relatable.

In the coming years, I spent nearly every summer in Montego Bay with my father's family. Kristina and Tomita's mom worked as a manager at a resort. I wandered the lobbies and thought of myself as those two blond kids from that Disney show. By the end of my first resort summer, the bartenders knew me by name and plopped down my usual order, which was a virgin strawberry daiquiri. As I wandered the resort during many of my summer days, Princess was at home looking after her many brothers and sisters. We were two siblings grappling with very different lives. The older we got, the more we became warped mirrors for the other—she for what a life in Jamaica could offer me and I for what life in the United States could give her.

That was why I always boarded the plane at the end of every summer with a knot in my stomach. I was beginning to realize that my life in Jamaica was filled with experiences only I could feel and never really convey. How could I tell my Black classmates that asked if lions ran wild in Jamaica that I loved the crackle of the radio from my grandmother's room in the evening or Sunday trips to the beach with my sister? How could I tell them that the slice of the island that I got was actually microscopic? How could I explain what that tiny little piece meant to me?

Manila, Cebu City, Binawi, Batad, Sagada,
Moalboal, Montalban, Philippines, 2017

Kevin pulled out the Android cell phone and propped it against a book as Lomo fumbled with the condom. My gaze shifted to Lomo, who was tall and slim, as he eased his body on top of mine. The room was dim past the closed curtains. Lomo's eyes closed and he grimaced. I gripped his thighs. Kevin smiled at me from the edge of the bed.

"Is that okay?" Lomo asked.

I nodded and coughed. The bedroom was dark and had a woody smell. When we stumbled into the room on that March night in 2017, I noticed it had furniture on all sides—dressers, a thin lamp, a dark-brown desk piled high with magazines, and a chair. The irony of being recorded as I lost my virginity was not lost on me. As I came, satisfied, some part of my mind also imagined an elderly white man somewhere wanking off to my brown frame on a porn site. I wondered, no, I dreaded whatever the video's title could be.

I'd come to the Philippines at the end of 2016 with Eli. Before the trip, we spent months meticulously planning it over the phone and envisioning a country-hopping video series of vlogs and short social justice documentaries. The trip gave me a North Star during a trying summer while working in Montana. Partway through my senior year of college, I became reacquainted with Colt. Too afraid to lose him again, I steered away from any conversations about whether he'd assaulted Adrian's cousin the summer before and leaned into our sexually murky friendship. That summer, it wasn't rare for Colt to call me drunkenly to describe in detail what he'd do to me if we were in bed together.

I partially wanted to go to the Philippines because I wanted the distinct chance to go very far away and choose, on a whim, when or if I'd come back. My many sleepless or drunken Montana nights made me realize that so much of my life until that point was about trying to stretch the person that I was to be extravagant or desirable enough to shatter someone else's inhibitions in a way that made me feel powerful.

■■■

As a child, I was always teased because of my larger head. The older I got, the more I internalized how my peers viewed me—a nerd, a know-it-all, an ugly duckling. My version of Blackness was worth mocking, whispering over in the hallways, and trying to reshape. It took me a long time to realize that confidence could be both trusting your worth and trusting the words of people that loved you enough to see you for who you are.

I stumbled through my freshman year of college too afraid to drink underage and with no concept of how to flirt. When a graduate student named Liam invited me to his dorm room during my fall semester, my heart raced as I climbed the stairs, laid down on his mattress, and accepted his offer for a massage. His father was a grand wizard of the KKK who had disowned him. Liam was balding and talked about how much thinner he'd been a few years ago. Initially bewildered and intrigued, I let his hands explore my body and his lips find mine. It wasn't until I left that the shame over my sexual desperation began to sink in.

Throughout college, so many parties were filled with straight white couples making out or queer white couples going home together. I graduated after months of waking up hungover on friends' couches and political organizing. The real world was so close and so very far away. I drank at the Smiling Skull Saloon and stumbled to Eli's home, which was closer to the bar than my apartment. For most of my senior year, I slept on Eli's floor or in bed next to him, the night swirling behind and above like some expansive black that wanted to swallow me up before I'd even been touched or really loved by another man. The frenzied teenager inside of me cried and fell into feverish dreams, where Eli reached for my forearm, held it, and brought me back to Earth. At my heart's weakest, I'd admit to Eli, "It doesn't make sense that everyone else gets to be loved and I don't."

Sometimes Eli didn't move. Sometimes he turned to face me.

"You're drunk and sad and I get that you're upset. Everyone finds someone eventually. That's how life works. Go to sleep. We have classes tomorrow."

The sound of his calmed breathing led to my snoring. Some nights I lay in bed next to him, hoping that some other part of

the universe could open up. Loneliness felt like a dying append-
age on my body, which would be followed by loss.

Months later, the eldest son of the owner of the newspaper
that I worked for passed away. A choir sang "Let It Be" by the
Beatles, which the eldest son had belted out at a karaoke bar a
year before. At the wake, Eli, his friends, and I went into my
boss's basement and drank whiskey. I was humbled, dressed in
black, and buzzing with the prospect of brotherhood.

■■■

Upon arrival to the Philippines on the evening of New Year's
Eve in 2016, I arranged to stay with Anthony on Couchsurfing,
a website that serves as a sort of Facebook for travelers. Anthony was exceedingly flexible, even to the point of offering to
pick me up from the airport, which made me feel looked after
as twenty-two-year-old in a brand new country.

"Hello, my friend," he said. "This is Nicole."

Anthony was tall, had a shaved head, and gave me a firm
handshake. He corralled Nicole and me into his friend's taxi.
Nicole, a thin, short woman, sat in the front seat. Anthony
turned to me and whispered, "She is not my wife. When you
meet my wife, this should stay between us."

Anthony taught me how to make pork adobo in his hot,
cement house. I squatted to poop into an open-face toilet in
his bathroom and had to look out for chickens that tried to
crawl through the holes in his walls. His television with few
channels reminded me of my grandmother's TV in Jamaica.
I appreciated the way he took up and navigated space in his

neighborhood of Taguig City. He chatted with the kids about basketball, the lady at the nearby store about rice prices, and the old men about their wives and girlfriends.

"What's your girlfriend's name?" Anthony asked me.

We were walking to the nearby market to buy chicken on my first official day there. The morning brought sweat-inducing humidity and I was fighting my hangover from the spectacle of the New Year's Eve celebrations the night before. I stayed up late chatting with the men in the neighborhood about the prospect of Donald Trump becoming president and laughed at the idea of him being assassinated. As the beer poured, I talked more and more about the racism and evils of America, all while attempting to be cognizant of the fact that I was entering this new country with its own history of colonization and political turmoil.

"I had a girlfriend, but you know how those things go . . ." I responded while fiddling with my phone.

"So you've had sex with many Black women? What are they like?"

"Black women are beautiful. Some of the most beautiful people in the universe," I retorted. "I kind of like to stick within my race."

Anthony nodded, satisfied with my answer, and I was relieved. It was a game I navigated while traveling—what parts of myself to reveal and what parts of myself to hold back. I was an American abroad and had more privilege than many of the people in the spaces that I was visiting. I also had drained my bank account to come here, was relying on the hospitality of my first host on Couchsurfing, and navigating being Black and gay abroad. It was not an impossibility that I could open up to Anthony and, afterward, be considered an anomaly, novelty, or spectacle to be questioned.

"But I have a secret to tell you," Anthony whispered the-atrically. "Nicole has a neighbor who has noticed you. I can leave the two of you alone in the apartment. You can have some Filipina pussy."

I coughed and fidgeted, telling Anthony some tale about the last vixen that had broken my heart and how I was incapa-ble of returning to my debonair ways. As we neared his house, I continued to sweat. Luckily, Anthony listened to me and didn't invite Nicole's neighbor to his house.

It was common for neighborhood men to come to my Couchsurfing host's door and demand that I hang out with them in the street. The neighborhood had long cement alleyways of stacked homes and tiny stores to buy cigarettes, groceries, or phone credit. All of my childhood summers in Jamaica made the ghetto and the laughter of old men as they smoked cartons of cigarettes a place of comfort. They enjoyed when I asked them to teach me Tagalog, the national language in the Philippines alongside English. Every misspoken phrase was a source of joy for them. They laughed harder when I made jokes about being bad at basketball, knowing Barack Obama, or how I'd once met LeBron James because I'd grown up in Cleveland.

"Oh, you are a negrito for sure if you like four by four," one man said to me in a bout of laughter.

I pulled money out of my pocket to contribute to the beer. He slapped my hand away.

"No, my friend. We buy you the beer."

During my first week, I paid fifty cents to crowd into a hot train for an hour-long ride to Manila's Chinatown. As I walked through streets of vendors, I was greeted by smiling women selling vegetables, and children crowded around me. This procession of being watched continued and continued and continued until the sweat dripping down my collar wasn't from the humidity, but my inability to be invisible and their inability to not consume me.

One woman shoved a dark-skinned baby toward me and said, "Father?" before laughing maniacally. I laughed, but my stomach turned. For three blocks, a gang of children followed me while giggling and pointing. I walked away briskly. I was called Wiz Khalifa, Bob Marley, and the Weeknd as the day wore on. On another trip to a mall with some of Anthony's friends, tourists stopped and asked to take photos with me, convinced that I was a basketball player.

Traveling with Eli complicated these interactions. As a fellow American, he could echo my confusion about why my skin and race meant so much to the people we passed in the streets. During a walk through downtown Manila, he trailed behind me and yelled, "Wow! Is that a Black dude?"

The calamity of my race followed where I went. Filipino culture manifested such hospitality and care, like my friend's family inviting Eli and me to eat a massive meal with them for his birthday. They loved hearing about our lives in the United States and asking about my baby dreadlocks, but couldn't grasp, rightfully so, from their end of the globe, that institutional racism still existed in America.

During our second month there, Eli and I traveled to various islands together. We arrived in Sagada after a long bus ride and browsed the small town for rooms. Any backpacker knows that a hot day and a massive bag will dampen your mood. My temper brewed as children pointed and laughed at me. The next day as I waited in Sagada's main downtown area while Eli used the bathroom, two girls from the group of laughing children found me.

Tan and cute, they hung on to each other and giggled as they edged closer. Through my weeks in the Philippines, I was careful when interacting with the kids to not trigger stranger danger from nearby adults.

"Negrito. Negrito," they said repeatedly.

They became obsessed with the Snapchat filters on my phone. After seeing them stare at my hair during the entire interaction, I offered to let them touch my budding dreadlocks. They plucked and prodded and laughed. When Eli returned, we boarded our bus. The beautiful mountains passed our view. I couldn't ignore the dark shadow moving through me.

I agreed to meet Eli in Quezon City at a club named Black Market a week later. After getting off at the wrong bus stop, I realized that my phone was dead. It was getting darker and my sense of direction was terrible. I also hated making people wait for me.

"My friend, are you lost? Where are you trying to go?"

I was circling the bus stop while trying not to eye the police officers in their marked car too often. I turned to the officer in the passenger seat, cautious as I edged closer.

"I'm trying to find this club that's nearby, but . . . my phone died."

"What club?"

Their car was turned off. The two men stared at me from the inside, clad in their uniforms. The sky was dark, the nighttime traffic in full swing. It was hot. I was stressed and I desperately wanted a drink. I told them the club's name and mentally kicked myself as I climbed into the car. The seat's leather felt worn against my fingers and I asked them to roll down the window.

"So you are going to this club? Do you do any drugs?"

"No sir," I replied. "But I do love Red Horse though."

The two men laughed as the city passed by us: large sky-scrapers with dying lights and half-filled jeepneys.

"We just ask because this club is known for having drug dealers there. Be careful because the police station has under-cover officers there. You wouldn't want to end up in any trouble."

Only a few weeks before, I'd been walking around China-town when an older shirtless Filipino man in front of an alleyway restaurant waved his hand and smiled at me. I edged closer and he held out of his hand as he offered to buy me weed. At the time, I was bewildered. So much of the news I'd read before arriving in the Philippines talked about the politics of Rodrigo Duterte.

After becoming president of the Philippines in June 2016, Rodrigo Duterte continued his penchant for being hard on crime and instituted an effective War on Drugs throughout the Philippines. As of January 2019, some estimates note that over thirty thousand killings of people suspected of selling or doing drugs have occurred throughout the country. Human rights or-ganizations and countless Filipino activists, however, state the number of extrajudicial killings must be much higher and the human rights violations drastically more severe.

"You are so young to be traveling alone. How are you able to afford this?"

"I try to travel on a small budget. I think it's good to see other cultures."

The two officers in the front glanced between each other and exchanged a smirk.

The passenger-seat officer spoke up next. "You ever been with a Filipina?"

"No. I haven't gotten the chance yet."

"There are some amazing women that you can buy for a few hours. It's a big thing that tourists like to do," the officer responded.

I felt their eyes on me in the rearview mirror. I thought of all the TV shows with travelers who met untimely ends. A queer, anarchist Black boy from Cleveland disappearing after climbing into a police car with a dead phone had never been one of them.

I stopped my voice from shaking as I talked. "I just got out of a breakup, so I'm taking things slow right now."

"And it's true what they say about Black men?"

I stopped chewing my gum. The officer in the passenger seat turned to look at me.

"How big is your dick?"

We neared the club. I spotted Eli on the sidewalk and rushed out of the back seat as quickly as I could. I bobbed to the music in Black Market and tried to hide my agitation as Eli and his new friend chuckled at my experience. In my entire life, my body had never radiated so intensely with this shade of anger that now made me stiffen every time I walked outside.

I avoided passing basketball courts filled with glistening teenagers. I dreaded meeting new people for fear that they'd fixate on my hair. On two different occasions in Manila, a random stranger gawked at my African features. When I video chatted with my mother, she commented on how dark I was getting. You have no idea, I thought.

Weeks later, a trans waitress chatted with Eli and me as we waited for a table. She looked me up and down before she said, "Is it true what they—once you go Black, you never . . . ?"

Eli and I exchanged knowing looks, then we left the restaurant immediately.

■ ■ ■

The Philippines was colonized by the Spanish from 1528 to 1898. Then the United States and Japan took control. During Spanish rule, mixed and lighter Filipinos were considered higher class while the field laborers were associated with having darker skin due to long hours in the sun. Over time the desire for lighter skin became a consequence of the colonial invasion, leading to the modern-day skin-bleaching industry prevalent throughout the island. In 2004, 40 percent of Filipino women reported using skin-bleaching products. Various reports predict that the global skin-bleaching industry will be valued at $24 billion by 2027.

At clubs, Eli, a philam (or mixed race), could be captivating and desirable. Women put their hands on his shoulder and smiled at him with warm eyes. Around gay men or people that liked to dress in drag, I could be followed, fawned after, and offered drinks, but only with the expectation that I was a conduit to Black culture. As Frank B. Wilderson III in *Afropessimism: An Introduction* stated, "What's important is that [the global attentiveness to Blackness] that is a process of psychic integration which is necessary for global community. So, one day there could be negrophobia in one psyche, the next day there could be negrophilia. One community could be completely, like teenage boys in the suburbs, negrophilic. Another community, like teenage boys in the deep south, could be completely negrophobic."

"So you are straight and still traveling with him, a gay man? That is so brave of you," a man in drag once said to Eli as we all left the bar at the same time. Then the man, brushing his hand against mine in the jeepney, asked me out on a date.

I would never admit to Eli or anyone else out loud, but part of my anger was at myself. I was jealous of the kind of attention that he got and the fact that he was so seemingly accepted in his home culture, something I had wrangled with in Jamaican and Black culture. The more that Eli connected with other Filipinos and regaled them with his journey of discovering his paternal side of the family's culture, the prouder and more disjointed I became. I sometimes glanced at him, grinning while we were out late at night, and felt a pang of guilt in my chest. He had his own cultural dilemmas to unravel as well. The knife's edge was jagged and I knew that my ability to see outside of myself was slipping.

After meeting up with Eli's childhood friend, Amihan, in Sagada, her family took us out to a bar. I threw back repeated cups of Red Horse beers while they bonded over the intricacies of Filipino culture. The slim woman onstage in red heels sang

"Wagon Wheel." The next morning, I was sure that someone had drained all the blood from my body in my sleep.

"Do you remember falling asleep at the bar?" Eli asked. "Why'd you drink so much?"

Eli carried my bags part of the way to the Sagada bus station. I stopped every block to sit on a stoop and tried to will away the spinning in my head. He handed me food. I turned it away. In the hangover delirium, I simply couldn't care if anyone gawked. My body escaped itself and I had to wait for it to come back.

In *The Souls of Black Folk*, W.E.B. Du Bois wrote, "It is a peculiar sensation, this double-consciousness, this sense of always looking at one's self through the eyes of others, of measuring one's soul by the tape of a world that looks on in amused contempt and pity. One ever feels his twoness,—an American, a Negro; two souls, two thoughts, two unreconciled strivings; two warring ideals in one dark body, whose dogged strength alone keeps it from being torn asunder."

By my third month in the Philippines, I could sense something breaking. I spent two weeks preparing for a trip to Montalban, the northernmost municipality in the province of Rizal, which would be our departure point to visit the Aetas villages of the northern Philippines.

"They are the aboriginals of the Philippines," a Black comrade in Seattle said when encouraging me to contact his friend, who helped build schools for the Aetas. "It's been a hard time for you. You should see some people that make you feel like home."

In the villages, the tether snapped. I stood, frozen and sweating, as the dark children in tattered clothes huddled around me while pointing and laughing. I forced my mind to center the privilege I had as someone with an American passport and travel-able income based on the resources at my disposal.

"Negrito!" they shouted, an echo of an echo, a tape repeating.

If I could have floated up and away from my body in that moment, I would have. Fading deep into the ether, a return to some ancient scene.

■ ■ ■

While in Moalboal for a week, Eli and I had flings with two different people in the same friend group. My lover for the week was a short bartender with a shaved head that poured Eli and me endless free drinks. Eli, an expert on my psyche, could read the way that I recoiled when the bartender placed his arm around me possessively or glanced at me dreamily at the bar. He could guess that I was going along with the illusion for a story to tell afterward.

On our last night in Moalboal, the bartender and I ran off to the beach. Under the shade of a rock overhang, we fondled each other's bodies. I took his cock into my mouth. I made him lose himself under my touch. I declined when he asked if I needed to cum. I put on my clothes quickly and walked away after the blow job was over. I paced the area around our hotel room while I waited for Eli to be done with his lover of the week. Once inside, I sat on the bed. Eli stared at me.

"Are you okay?"

I took off my shoes and concentrated on breathing. The room was dark. I listened for the ocean water outside and hated the silence that returned.

"It wasn't fun," I sighed. "I didn't have fun and when he finished I didn't want him to touch me. I didn't think I could . . ."

"You couldn't what?"

"I just didn't like the idea of him touching me and trying to get me off," I spat out. "It all feels like a fucking game. You go out. You pick someone up. You give them your body and then what do you get in return? What do I get back?"

Eli leaned forward a bit from where he sat. I could see the wheels spinning in his mind as he tried to decipher what I was saying. It felt like he was holding a flashlight inches from my face and aiming the beam of light into me. Once the images and sensations started, they couldn't stop.

I was back in the Beauvais Airport outside of Paris earlier that year, walking through security, feeling like I should run back, fall into bed with the boy I'd met there, and release myself to him. My body, a live wire again as I walked away. Too afraid to stand my ground in the way that I should have.

"I lied," I confessed.

"What did you lie about?"

My body slackened. I edged farther back onto the bed and rested against the wall.

"You know how I told you that I lost my virginity when I went to France? To that dude, Enzo?"

Eli nodded.

"I was tired of telling the same story. I was tired of being the boy that crawls into their friend's room and cries about how lonely they are. I wanted something different."

There is the longstanding belief that gay people are inherently promiscuous. Whether it stems from the medical and psychological community deeming homosexuality a mental illness or religious fervor, the belief persists. The other side of the coin, however, is that no one hands a young gay person in a homophobic family a guide to sex, sensuality, and boundaries. I had been fumbling through the whole mess of it and getting flashbacks to my mother trying to convince me that anal sex would ruin my body. Finding love and a good lay could become an expression of liberation for queer people. But if I hadn't fucked or been fucked, could I really feel liberated in the way that I wanted to? Was my body still a cage?

I'd learned to be proud to be queer, but the next battle was how to manifest desire moment by moment. I wanted what bell hooks wrote about in *All About Love: New Visions*, "In order to change the lovelessness in my primary relationships, I had to first learn anew the meaning of love and from there learn how to be loving."

Virginity, for such a long time to me, felt like a threshold. It was a boundary that proved that I was a part of the waking world, a bridge from how coming out conditions us to seek acceptance to the way fucking makes us feel seen. Quite simply, I could only chuckle at who my first kiss's father was or feel ashamed. Coming into my sexuality, in many ways, felt like being swallowed up by people that I couldn't really trust to know if they wanted me.

"Who wants to be the loser that goes to France, meets a boy, and doesn't lose his virginity? Who wants to be the boy going to parties and watches everyone else kiss and fuck and experience? When do I get what I want?"

Eli moved across the room and sat next to me.

"If you didn't like this guy, why didn't you just say no?"

"Why should I pass up what I don't get offered that much?"

He gave me a knowing glance and I exhaled. I tried to concentrate on colors shading my vision in the dark room. I tried to place myself anywhere but there, which was where that light-headed feeling washed over me when I was walking the streets of Manila and all too noticeable. I tried to fixate on everything that I'd held on to and pushed it inward. Burying it all inside of myself meant that at least I had armor, that I was not powerless, and that at my strongest, I didn't need validation.

Then, just like that, I let the armor go and I told him. How a supposed friend had moved his hands over my body. How his passion hadn't felt like knives of something hot and good, but bugs crawling over my skin. How I'd reshaped myself to be casual around him when I couldn't wash the imprint of him off of me in the shower. Then how he'd found me again in my room and then again with his letter, which ached with desperation and suburban rebellion. What a stupid metaphor I'd fallen into. Just more white hands colonizing Black flesh.

I just want you to be happy. I never meant to hurt you. Actually I admire you. But weren't those words just a variation of what my mother and father had tried to ensnare me in? Manipulation disfigured and dressed up as love.

After France earlier that year, I visited Adrian in Budapest. Thinking that all the wounds from the previous summer in Yellowstone had healed, we got drunk one night and in the middle of me talking about my romantic insecurities, he tried to kiss me. In the elevator going up to his apartment, where he was allowing me to crash in an extra room, he leered at me. I was the prey that had fallen into his trap again. I rejected his many advances. I pushed my luggage up against the inside of my door, stayed up until five a.m., and decided that if it came down to it, I would beat the blood out of his body if he tried to seduce me again.

"I don't want to be that scared person huddled in that room anymore," I said to Eli. "Sometimes I can't tell if I'm hiding from him, myself, or every boy I go to bed with."

Eli's expression turned studious, which made him even more handsome. Then a small smile surfaced on his face. My heart, a bit more alive, moved in my chest.

"You don't have to lie to be some other person to be my friend or anyone else's. I'm your friend and that means it's my job to tell you that you can say no and be whoever you want and who you are happens to be the guy that went on a cross-country road trip with me. You organize and demonstrate and write and you're pretty lazy as far as exercising goes. Don't give up any of that because there's parts of your life that you wish were different. You are who you are for a reason and that's nothing to be ashamed of."

■ ■ ■

It was through my Tinder date with Ben, who was a tall and long-limbed model, that I met Paul during my last month in the Philippines. For the date, Ben and I went to a restaurant, talked, and ended the evening cordially. Afterward, Ben was nice enough to invite Eli and me out to a club that he worked at as a doorman. The club's ceiling was filled with intersecting tube lights, and a DJ mixed records on the stage. I avoided the overpriced bar and drank outside of a nearby 7-Eleven. Eli and I laughed while dancing freakishly to the gothic techno music.

We were sweaty by the time we met Ben's friends outside. Paul was short, of medium build, and had dark hair. I often tried to meet stoic people with an overwhelming warmth, so I smiled at Ben's friends too much out of nervousness. I liked that Paul didn't turn away from my gaze.

A week later I saw Paul again at the same club. While Eli was outside chatting up new friends, I sat on a couch alone and peered out at the other fashionable queer people at the bar. I liked the idea of sitting at a gay bar and not staring at my phone or waiting for someone's attention. Eventually, a tall Chinese man sat down next to me and said nothing. I glanced at him and then smiled before leaning in.

"How's your night going?"

He glanced my way, his eyes slightly obscured by the black hair falling from beneath his cap. I could tell he was trying not to grin.

"Just hanging out with some friends."

I inched a little closer on the couch and looked at him more firmly, then said, "I just want to know because it's important. Did you sit here because you think I'm cute?"

He waited, then replied, "Yeah."

"Do you think that I think you're attractive?"

Within moments, I was making out with this stranger. I suggested we take our escapades to the bathroom. He obliged. In the bathroom stall, we chuckled and pushed ourselves harder against each other's clothed bodies. We eventually decided to leave the bathroom and go to his house. I realized that I had to tell Eli, who had come with me, that I was leaving.

"What's this guy's name?" Eli asked.

"I don't know and I don't care. This is hot as fuck."

I couldn't, however, find the handsome stranger when I went back inside to look for him. So Eli and I got drunker, high off of the night's energy. It was three a.m. when we agreed to go out for a late-night meal with Ben, Paul, and their friends. They led us to a restaurant with seating in the parking lot. I sat across from Paul.

He pinned me down immediately when he asked, "So what have you learned here in the Philippines?"

His gaze sobered me and I realized I wanted to meet his eyes with my own gaze any chance that I got. It wasn't just that he'd asked a question, but he'd asked something that most people didn't care to know. Friends liked to ask what delicious foods you've eaten abroad or the most striking things that you'd seen. What I had learned was a different story, the important story.

"Anything more than a few words of Tagalog?"

I smirked at his snarky follow-up question and leaned back into my chair. I decided to play ball with him.

"I've learned we don't always get what we want, no matter where we are. The simplest things are usually the hardest."

"And that's okay? For you?"

I looked across the table again. Eli was grabbing someone's hand and telling them a joke earnestly. Ben was on his phone texting. The drag queen that had come along with us pulled a small bottle of liquor out of her purse and laughed. I turned back to Paul.

"For a Black boy traveling, I don't know."

With each question, I could feel Paul edging closer to me. There was something warm and wild about how easy it was for both of us to just unload. He asked me about why I wrote. I told him that the best part of it was finishing a piece, whether it be a poem, novel, or essay, with concrete certainty that it was meant to be in the world. That feeling had saved me more times than I could count.

"What do you like to do?" I asked him.

"I like clothes. I like collecting clothes and showing a sort of dreamlike reality through them. It's all a way of expressing something. Darkness. Childhood. Loss," he replied. "And what about you? What do you plan to do here?"

I imagined all the walking, the heat, and the steam rising off of the food carts on street corners. My face grew hot at the thought of another child laughing at me. I started to frown.

"I think I'm tired of being angry. I'm tired of ... feeling like I could disappear and be eaten alive at the same time."

Paul let me talk, and in talking I found a new kind of healing that was different from what I felt with Eli or any other friends. I wanted to divulge these things to Paul, but what I wanted even more was for him to reveal the difficult parts of himself to me. The past weeks had planted a cynicism in me, but maybe this new feeling could take that away. He kept his gaze on me and for those two hours, the rest of the table disappeared.

There are countless romantic-film montages about potential lovers wrestling over the mistakes and opportunities encapsulated in their first meeting—waiting by the phone, checking their email, stalking the other person's social media accounts, and replaying the scenario repeatedly. With Paul, there was no obsessive montage period. Knowing that my spirit, not my Blackness, was at the forefront while speaking to him was good enough for me.

His questions led me to the internet and research. I needed a break from the emotional bedlam that the Philippines had become. I contacted several friends and found out that volunteering at hostels was a possibility. I talked to Eli over breakfast at a nearby restaurant days later and told him the news.

"South Korea?" he asked.

The small restaurant where we were had five tables with patrons spilling onto the sidewalk. I scooped rice and pork adobo onto my plate. We passed a cold soda between the two of us quickly.

"There's a hostel there that I can volunteer at for twenty hours a week in exchange for a bed and food," I replied. "I have enough money for a plane ticket there and not much else."

The morning heat always hit like a wave. Although I'd become used to the sweat, I still wasn't used to how the sweat made all the sights and smells stick to your skin. Manila buzzed all around us. I realized this was the beginning of one thing and a goodbye to something else.

Eli stuttered slightly as he responded, "You'll be okay? You, you won't—"

My heart warmed, so I stopped him and stared down his worry.

"I'll be okay."

▪ ▪ ▪

I would lose my virginity to Lomo and Kevin a few nights later as Kevin's cell phone recorded while propped against a stack of books. The Manila sun was bright and as I walked away, every smell attached to my body. I would never truly become a part of Manila, but Manila and my moments there had become a part of me. Anthony, teary eyed as he hugged me, made me promise to come back. Eli made jokes about how nice it would be to have the bedroom that we rented together to himself.

We went out to Today x Future, a new bar, on my last night. It was cramped and narrow with shimmering silver walls. Everyone stumbled in each other's space in drunken kindness. I looked around at the crowd and drank to commemorate my new body. I exchanged short hellos with Paul when he showed up, but tried to keep my distance. I stood outside alone and smoked a cigarette while looking out at the street. Eli came close and whispered in my ear, "What are you doing dude? You're wasting time."

"What are you talking about?"

"Paul just talked to me and I can tell he's so into you."

There are times when there is no rope strong enough to keep our reservations within their boundaries. My feet carried me to Paul where he stood by the bar. The energy between us was palpable. He snuck a glance at me and smirked. I liked when he smirked.

"Ben is going to be pissed if he sees us talking to each other," Paul admitted.

"Why's that?"

He didn't even need to look at me. The answer moved between us. He and Ben were best friends. The potential betrayal was obvious, but part of me didn't care. We ordered drinks and stood next to each other, glancing across the narrow room at all the people smoking, talking, and savoring this night, the only night. If this country or any country was going to change, then it was the youth that would likely lead the way.

"Are you sad to leave?" he asked.

I looked at him, a bit surprised.

"Eli told me earlier," he revealed.

"Sad?" I said as I glanced to Eli, who was chatting animatedly with someone near the front porch, then back to Paul, "I don't think sad is the right emotion."

"What is?"

"I feel like I've been carrying this person on my back and the only way to get him off, to see what I've learned is to move on. I can't walk around feeling like an animal anymore."

Paul nodded, then took a long sip of his drink.

"It feels good though," I said. "Like I took some control that I somehow lost along the way."

A long moment passed. I tried to read Paul's silence. I didn't like that he was avoiding my gaze. My chest felt heavy and light at the same time.

"Why don't we do something fun tonight?"

"When is your birthday," he responded.

"Um . . . June 30."

He nodded, snickered, and finished his drink. When he spoke again, his voice had an edge.

"So that's it."

I froze and then asked, "What are you talking about?"

"You remind me of this boy that I dated. Dated him for a while and," he sighed, "he left without a real explanation and it's messed me up since. He was a Cancer too."

I was taken aback, bewildered by the fact that my mere presence could have triggered him or catalyzed an unraveling. Now I noticed it. He was sinking into the wall, trying to lose himself in the calamity around us. I looked at him and wanted him to look back.

That voice in the pit of my stomach was yelling at me. No longer was I a Black boy gripped with the dilemma of living with Blackness abroad. I was a man that had met someone, shared the kind of gaze that rattled cages, and now I knew the truth. What was the point of feeling so deeply, putting in so much hope if you don't get close to anything that you expected? How did life move from an endless act of waiting for love to appreciating love in all its forms?

I wanted to lean over Paul, stir his insides with my gaze, and kiss him on the mouth softly and then heavily. He would reach for my belt, pull my center into him, and then melt. Quite simply, I wanted everything. Everything, however, was too far away. So I settled for now.

"I don't know you that well and I don't want to assume anything that feels invasive to you, but you should know that I think you're an amazing person. You're smart and you ask really tough questions. You've made me feel like more of a person than I have felt in weeks. It doesn't have to be me that you open up to, but I hope you know that you deserve whatever you're looking for."

Paul nodded and eventually I had to walk away. I half listened to conversations with Eli. I drank more Red Horse beer than I should have. I made small talk with Ben and Paul, trying to urge them to go out for food. Ben was disinterested. Paul said "maybe" with a reserved purse of the lips. I could tell that he knew Ben was annoyed.

I kept thinking, What would be so bad about Paul kissing me tonight?

Paul shook my hand goodbye and then set off the dynamite with his words when he said, "Good luck on your travels. You're a beautiful person. It was nice meeting you."

I'm beautiful and it was nice to meet me, I thought the next morning as I stared at my filled bags with quiet discontent. Eli watched periodically from the door. I ate almost nothing for breakfast, called a cab to the airport, rolled the windows down, and tried to memorize the city's scent of smog and dust and sweat. My heart soared at the sight of men zooming down highways on the backs of motorcycles, a moment that I'd experienced myself during my first month there.

■■■

"People are staring at you so much," a friend in South Korea whispered to me as we walked to the bars at night.

I shrugged as an answer and got plastered for the fourth time that week. Busan, South Korea, had many more neon lights than the Philippines and young people with long legs and ashen skin. I walked past the red tents on street sides, with the smell of fish wafting into the post-midnight air.

I skated by the beach and smoked weed in obscure tattoo shops. I let curious Koreans touch my hair in exchange for drinks until it had been over a week since I'd bought myself a drink. Sometimes women under the strobe lights stared at me and giggled to one another, certainly curious about the lanky Black boy. I decided that if I was going to be lost and swallowed alive out in the world, then I'd at least get something for myself out of it.

I stole most of my meals and alcohol during the trip, even corralling hostel guests to help me steal by serving as distractions until an elderly 7-Eleven worker stopped me. She grabbed for my arm and I shoved her away, darting through the maze of the underground subway system.

I arrived at an airport in China for an eighteen-hour layover during my journey back to the United States. With only seven dollars in my pocket, I stole trail mix from the airport's stores, griped at all of the websites that were blocked, and tried to sleep on my stiff bag as different parts of the airport around me closed. In the middle of sleep, a foot poked me awake. I looked up to see a Chinese couple standing over me.

"You take photo with my wife," the man said.

"No. No. No," I muttered, not even mustering the energy to move. The man nudged my bag. Instead of lunging at him, I pinned my eyes shut and waited for them to leave.

I flew back to Ohio on a sunny spring day. My mother's face changed when she looked at me for the first time in months. She looked disappointed, almost angry, like I had deprived her child of what could make him plump, healthy.

"You weren't eating, were you?" she asked smartly.

I lied, went to the bathroom, peeled off my clothes, and stared in the mirror almost in shock. I realized what exactly had been lost beyond body weight as I plucked at my taut skin. I had run out of money and stopped eating some of my meals while I'd been gone, but I didn't dare complain. So many people had so much less than me. I had known for years that travel wasn't always meant to be easy or digestible to people that ask the age old question, "How was it?" after you are done. What I hadn't known was that travel and anti-Blackness can shave down entire parts of your body and mind and lead to fear setting the boundaries for what we believe is possible.

After stepping into a church in Charleston, South Carolina, in 2015, Dylann Roof opened fire on churchgoers and their children at the end of Bible study. When he came upon Polly Sheppard, Roof stopped firing and told her, "I'm not going to shoot you. I'm going to leave you here to tell the story."

In Roof's logic, Black people largely exist as an antagonistic force to whiteness. In Ms. Sheppard's logic, it is possible for Black people to be more than how we survive our suffering. Beyond white terror and what it produces is the world-ending possibility that we Black people own ourselves and it is only the bullet that cements the lie, the shackle, the cell, the noose, the racial slur, and our world's often reductive view of Black people into reality. Both truth and lies can separate or bind us.

"What did you expect?" I could hear my mother saying as I stared at myself in the mirror, "They don't got many of us over there."

But even with that truth, I couldn't rub away the good. The good was staring up at the fireworks shooting through the sky on New Year's Eve, holding on to a friend as we hurtled down the highway on a motorcycle under a purple sunset, singing karaoke with Eli and Amihan at Guihon Resto Bar in Kinakin, our bellies full of fried fish and rice, or waking up and stumbling down to the beach after a night of cheap drinking to talk with other travelers. There was gazing into Paul's face and Eli listening to me in that dark room. Both felt just like finding home in a distant place.

Traveling to the Philippines allowed me to understand that the world could define me in so many and so few ways.

Yellowstone National Park, United States, 2014

At the start of the summer, Kyle was my only friend in Yellowstone. I met him the year before in college. He was another writer that frequented Donkey Coffee and wore beanie hats to top off his gaunt features. I tagged along with him and his friends for the first week or so in Yellowstone and quickly realized they gave off an air of hipness that made them feel superior to our other coworkers. There was also the white guy in his group that wore sunglasses all the time and used glue to hold his handlebar mustache in place. All of my other co-workers were mostly college students on summer vacation, long-term season workers, adrenaline junkies, and something in between.

Kyle proposed the summer job in Yellowstone to me and promised how easy the work would be as a housekeeper. Instead I was assigned a job in the cafeteria, which gave me drastically different hours than Kyle.

There was also the debacle of my last bus ride to Wyoming just a few weeks before. I was one of the last two passengers who attempted to board the bus and was not let on.

"It's full," the large Black bus driver said gruffly before shutting the door in my face.

I was given a new ticket for the next bus to Jackson Hole, Wyoming, but had to wait eighteen hours to board again. I stepped outside of the small, narrow bus stop and looked out at the rising sun. A small thrill moved through me. This is what travel is about, I thought.

For the next twelve hours, I roamed the handful of blocks that comprised the downtown area. There was a hotel that had a lobby that was too small for me to inconspicuously hang out in. It was early June, but a man that looked like Santa Claus was the only other person at a cafe that I posted up at a for a few hours. It neared noon when I called my mother. I roamed the aisles of an antique store while giving her updates on my travels.

"You're where?"

"I'm in this small town and I have to wait for the next bus. I'm fine though. I just had lunch."

My mother kissed her teeth. Then a long moment of silence.

"This is a stupid idea. You must be trying to mess up your future."

My heart stumbled a beat. I forced myself to sit down in the closest chair. I'd grown up knowing that my mother had a short fuse. I'd also grown up highly aware of how often her short fuse exploded in the exact moments I'd wanted her support.

"It's just a summer job. I'm going to work and save money and meet new people. What's wrong with that?"

"You want to hang out with white people you don't know," she spat back. "Tell them your business and get yourself in all kinds of trouble? You a damn idiot. You—"

"Why are you acting like I'm doing something wrong? Lots of people take jobs in other states for a few months in the summer. It's not a bad thing!"

I scanned the antique store and looked for any wayward glances in my direction. The room felt hotter than before. I walked toward the door.

"You're reckless, just like your father, and look what happened to him. Good luck."

In my life, that might have been the first time that I hung up on my mother. I waited longer and boarded my final bus to Wyoming, fighting back the heat building behind my eyes.

As a child, I became accustomed to my mother's lackluster anecdotes about my biological father anytime I asked questions about him. I would never admit it to her, but it hurt me deeply that I didn't even know his favorite color and that there hadn't been enough sentimentalism in his death to encourage her to tell me such details. I learned over time, however, that the signs of a man that I'd never really known could be navigated, slowly. Now I was the farthest away from home that I had ever been. Her verbal spit on my father's grave led me to a decision. I refused to be a boy simply stumbling into a dead father's legacy.

My Yellowstone job entailed waking up before sunrise, dragging myself to a cold shower, and standing behind the hot buffet line in a cafeteria. By eleven p.m., when most of my last shifts ended, I wandered back to the employee dorms to find Kyle and his friends drinking while crammed into one of their rooms. Dog tired, I plopped down next to Kyle, grabbed his pint of Black Velvet Whisky, and sipped.

"Where the hell do you get so much alcohol?" I asked him after one of my first nights of work.

"You just gotta know where the cameras are," he replied with a wink.

The next day, Kyle and I left lunch early to go on a walk to the general store. Kyle complained about all his new friends and even called them shallow. He was dissatisfied with his old friends as well. He chain-smoked and looked like some Beatnik character. He spoke while looking out at the shoreline of Yellowstone Lake. "Even though I'm the reason they all came from Ohio to work here, they don't seem very grateful."

I was contemplating whether to tell Kyle that he needed to be patient or pull the stick out of his ass when we waltzed into the liquor aisles of the general store. I opened my mouth to speak when I saw him slip a pint bottle into his jacket. Once outside the door, I wiped the sweat from my brow. Kyle handed one of the pints to me with another wink.

"Like I said, you gotta know where the cameras are."

Although my heart raced and I could only think of myself fleeing the park rangers as we walked away, I had to admit that I was glad that Kyle showed me a way to ease the stress of my job. My hopes for the summer included what sweat-inducing work would teach me and befriending odd characters. The fantasy quickly lost its romance. The pipes in our dorms clanked, often waking us up at night. The employee lunch that we were served consisted of leftovers. As a cafeteria buffet server and cashier, I often had to deal with buses filled with hundreds of elderly tourists flooding the cafeteria on a weekly basis. They joined the line, bleary eyed and clutching their coupons. Once a white woman approached, squinted as I pointed at chicken, and then said, "Do you have any roast beef?"

I griped, thinking of all the expressions of the workers at the resort that my aunt worked at in Jamaica and how they turned away from tourists to hide their annoyance Despite working close to fifty hours a week, my checks usually amounted to no more than $400 after housing, food costs, taxes, and insurance were taken out. I was grimacing while examining my first paycheck when I met Colt. We were sitting in the lobby and talking to the dorm administrator about his many seasons of work at resorts. Colt nudged me in the side and asked if I wanted to go on a walk to find some beer.

With light-blond hair and pale skin, Colt looked like a body covered in white paint with two blue orbs for eyes. He spoke with a small lisp and everything he wore shone against him. I liked the way that he moved, muscles pulling against his sturdy frame, and how he singled me out. Colt was also from the Midwest, but a little less traveled than me. He finished high school and spent a gap year working odd jobs in Michigan until someone told him about the amazing opportunity to work across the country for a summer.

"I broke up with my girlfriend and came out here," he confided that first night.

We walked through the stacks of cabins, which were empty in preparation for the beginning of the summer resort season, and searched the shadows for the shapes of wild animals. He led me to an empty cabin room, opened the window from the outside, climbed in, and exited with a six-pack of beer in hand.

"I found these while cleaning today," he said as he tossed me one. "Our little secret."

So began our ritual of talking during long walks at night as we sipped alcohol, looked out for stray bison in the shadows, and unloaded our insecurities onto each other. Aside from Colt and Kyle, I started to make other friends too. Sky was a frizzy-haired high school graduate that had never been away from home before. Caleb had come all the way from California, worked with me in the cafeteria, and liked to keep her head afloat above all the employee gossip happening at all hours. Colt's roommate, Adrian, was a political science major that loved to talk politics with me. I met Duncan during my second week while he read a '70s Black-crime comic book on the employee dorm's front stoop. We talked about movies and politics into the late-night hours.

It was fun to steal pints from the general store, then laugh with Colt and Sky as we snuck into the employee pub after work. I ignored my mother's calls, still hurt by the words that she'd spat at me on the phone a few weeks earlier during my journey out west. For the first time in my life outside of school, I had traveled somewhere and found a makeshift family. Even though I would have never said it aloud, it felt like some mystical and very adult part of me was developing. I hoped this additional skin could become a kind of armor to help guide me into adulthood.

The next week, I was drinking with Adrian, his cousin, and Kyle's friends when someone knocked at the door. The room fell silent as everyone's faces slackened and they set their beers down. A park ranger stepped inside. I wondered why I hadn't thought to hide in the closet just ten seconds before.

"I'm going to need to see everyone's IDs."

Everyone but Adrian, his cousin, Beth, and I were over twenty-one. It rained as the park ranger placed Adrian and me outside of his car. We shivered. I held Adrian close and whispered repeatedly, "This isn't a big deal. You don't have to cry."

The park ranger separated the two of us. After bringing me inside to the warm dorm hallway, he stared, pursed his lips, and placed his hands on his hips. The outside drizzle collected on his mustache as we stood in the hall

"Are you going to tell me where you got that alcohol?"

I kept my arms crossed and tried to not feel too small as I avoided staring at his ranger badge too much. It perplexed me how much time the rangers must have had on their hands to prioritize a bunch of rowdy twenty-year-olds in a dorm room. He handed me a citation with a court date and left. The next night, Colt and I went for another walk. I was tired from the day's work. The two of us sat on a blanket on a ledge that overlooked Lake Yellowstone. Colt started talking about how grand the summer was becoming, how much he was learning, and mostly, what it meant to be away from his ex-girlfriend.

I interjected, "I thought you were seeing some girl in housekeeping though . . ."

He blushed a little and nodded before handing me the bottle of peach schnapps. I held the bottle in my hands and made no move to open it. He noticed.

"Getting a little drunk won't kill you. It might actually help because of how stressed you are."

The liquid went down thick and too sweet, but I decided that I didn't mind. I took a few swigs, then handed the bottle back to him.

"What are you thinking about?" he asked.

I pulled my knees close to me and stared out at Yellowstone Lake. I was four weeks into my summer and a part of my life in this new place had already imploded. I couldn't shake going to breakfast that morning and sitting with all the other people that had been caught by the rangers the night before. One thing became obvious to me very quickly.

"I don't think it matters to them the same way that it matters to me," I told Colt.

"What do you mean?"

"My stepdad is in prison again. I'm in university mostly on scholarship. I don't even really have a family to fall back on in a lot of ways and . . ."

I took the bottle from Colt again and drank until my eyes started to water. The image from that morning ran through my mind. Handlebar-mustache guy was laughing, staring up at me with crinkled eyes, and patting me on the back as I sat down. When he joked at the table about all of us being in the same club, my stomach tightened into a knot that I'd been trying to loosen all day.

"And what?" Colt inquired.

They're white, I thought.

"At breakfast, they laughed like it was nothing," I replied instead.

A silence swept over us. I peeked at Colt a few times from the side of my gaze and wondered why he didn't inquire more from me. Then I noticed his hand, which was resting on the blanket next to mine. I wondered how it would feel to be touched by that hand or to feel it move you in the darkness.

Pushing the thought away, I drank again and decided that I was entitled to a bit of unraveling.

I pressed on and said, "It's just fucked up. We get handed a life and told to follow all these rules . . . Where does it get us? I came all the way here to find something and all I ended up learning is that I might end up like my dad or my stepdad. Just bleeding out somewhere or in some cell. Maybe she was right."

I told Colt about the phone conversation with my mother, my hands feeling like giant weights at my side. When his face softened after hearing my mother's words, I knew that he needed to know the whole truth. So I willed myself to him.

I told him about 1995 and the shadow that my father's death cast over my life; how he was flung from some back seat on a roadside as he bruised and bled, under a stack of bodies by some unmarked grave, or relegated to photographs. If I was reckless enough to get caught underage drinking, maybe I was also destined to be reckless enough to end up dead or worse, like him, a cautionary tale.

A long silence followed. In my dizziness, I hoped Colt could feel the same nameless and chest-unwinding emotion that I did.

"Look. I'm not trying to make a move or anything," he muttered.

He wrapped his arms around my waist and hugged me so that his chest rested on my shoulder. Suddenly it felt like I'd grabbed onto an electrical wire, then was dumped into the lake water resting right in front of us. The jolt was so powerful that I didn't worry how fast my heart was beating. I rested my hand on Colt's back, looked out at the dark sky filled with endless stars, and realized something. No man had ever touched me in the way that Colt just had.

I exhaled and tried to count the reasons that everything might end up alright.

■■■

It wasn't long after the night with Colt while sitting on the blanket that he, Sky, and I decided to go camping. With so many people in our dorm caught for underage drinking, we thought that it was better to drink out in the wilderness. The next week, we all had the same night off and packed up Colt's car. During the hour drive to the campsite, we stopped at general stores and picked up booze along the way. Our debauchery took a little too long, so by the time we reached the campsite, the sun was setting. We ambled around while looking for firewood and clutching our prized pints of liquor. Sky fell into a bush and scraped her legs. Colt and I played music from my cheap Bluetooth speaker, which rested on a log. Sky passed out a few feet from the fire. In my gaze, I mostly made out how the orange floating up from the fire pit coated Colt's pale skin.

We stared at each other, trying to drink up each other's bodies with our eyes. Feeling the breathlessness and excitement, he spoke in a small grin, "We should get naked."

Soon enough, I was holding Colt's body, pressing my lips softly against his chest, and moving downward as he breathed. I licked and pawed and pulled at him in the firelight. He let me sit on his lap as I tried to stare into his eyes as deeply as possible. The mountain spun around us. Then it all faded into blackness, where I hoped to give as much of myself to Colt as I could.

The next morning, we all awoke hungover. I skimmed the dirt for my phone and finally found it. On the car ride back to Yellowstone Lake, Sky stuck her head out the window. I knew that she was trying not to vomit. The whole morning, Colt and I spoke to each other but failed to look each other in the eyes. Twenty minutes into our car ride, he looked at me in the rear-view mirror.

"Did you give me a blow job last night?"

We laughed the rest of the ride back to the employee dorms and told our coworkers about the niceties of our trip. It felt good to end an affair with a boy and to not look back wistfully.

I went to court with all of my white coworkers and accepted my punishment alongside them, taking an online class about legal and responsible alcohol consumption. Adrian and I bonded as we sped through the lessons together. I found him fine enough to hang out with, but sometimes disliked how he spoke as if we shared the same political world, despite the fact that he'd come from a middle-class family.

"I think he might have a crush on you," Sky mentioned one day when she caught me walking back to the dorm.

I shivered at her suggestion. That night, we got drunk. It was more of the same of sharing pints of stolen booze, running around the dorms, and dressing up in each other's clothes. Sky, Colt, Adrian, and I fell asleep in the room that Adrian and Colt shared. I awoke in the middle of the night, pressed against Adrian. His leg draped over mine. Then his arm. His lips found me. I thought the moaning was coming from some other place until I realized that the noise was coming from his mouth. I pulled myself away and said I had to go to the bathroom.

Even showering after work the next day didn't get rid of the strange feeling in the pit of my stomach, the same spot that had been excited when I'd touched Colt on Shadow Mountain. I stayed by myself and avoided drinking with Colt, Adrian, Sky, and our other friends for the next two nights. Adrian sent me nightly text messages to ask if I wanted to hang out, but I promptly ignored them. On the third night, Adrian found me in my room while he was drunk and crawled into my bed. It was impossible to move as I listened to the silence of him using my body, or maybe the silence was me. It was shocking how desperate he was to find my quiet flesh.

The next day, Adrian texted me and demanded that I find him immediately. I found him in a cabin room with his house-keeping cart unused in the corner. He sat silently on the bed next to his cousin, Beth.

"What's going on?" I asked.

"Colt raped me last night," Beth replied.

The warmth left the room until the lightness in my head made me realize I should sit down as well. The bed creaked under the weight of a third person and I gazed ahead at the dust glowing and floating in the sunlight. I hated it, how quickly the words left my mouth after having lived a lifetime of men taking advantage of the women around me.

"What do you need, Beth?"

Upon Beth's instructions, Adrian and I tried to take her back to her room to help her pack. On the way there, we were stopped by someone from HR who corralled her into their car "to talk." Adrian and I stared at each other, left in a cloud shot up from the car speeding away. Next we went to his room and cleared away the cans of beer from the night before. Colt looked at us, asked us questions, and then turned red in the face when we ignored him. It took only an hour or so before the rumors spread like wildfire around the dorms. I was the third person to be questioned by the rangers. In the middle of my interview, Colt stormed in and dropped a purse on the ground.

"That was hers. She left it in my truck yesterday when we were all out having fun," he said before storming out. He had refused to look me in the eyes.

If Colt hadn't mentioned it, the memory wouldn't have run through my mind: Colt, Sky, Adrian, Beth, and I shouting like maniacs as we stripped off our clothes and steered our boat around a section of the lake. We were high on the prospect of our brilliant summer of shitty work and debauchery ending. I snapped photos of everyone on my stolen disposable camera. It felt eerie to have such a fond memory so certainly defiled.

An hour later, Tara, one of my cafeteria coworkers, pulled me into her dim room with closed curtains. She stood by the door and said, "You should sit down."

I sat on the bed. We waited, almost like a standoff, before she found the courage to speak after sitting next me.

"Colt left his room last night after what he did to Beth and he wandered around, even tried to sneak into some other girl's room. He scared the shit out of everyone."

I buried my face in my hands and tried to breathe through the heat taking over my body. I walked to the lobby with red eyes and ignored everyone's questions as I passed. Colt was parked in front of the employee dorms and throwing his bags into the trunk of his car. I thought of the blanket, of Colt's hands wrapped around my waist, and how I felt by the dying fire as we pressed our bodies into each other. For so long, I'd convinced myself that those moments defined my summer. Now I realized that those moments, which had softened me, only made my flesh more tender as the summer's knife dug in deeper.

I had loved someone and wanted them to touch my body, explode me, upend me in a way that they had violated in someone else. This proved that my desires could be monstrous and were walking around, looking and acting like people.

I left Yellowstone a beaten-up mess while jammed in the filled back seat of my coworker's car. We had decided weeks before to go on a road trip to California. I was tired of being exploited at my job and of drinking through all the intensity. I wanted to give something back to myself. I started talking to my mother again and gluing together the not-so-accurate idea of me that she had.

"California?" she said over the phone.

"For about a week and then I'll fly back to Ohio. I'll have a few days to spare before classes."

She didn't criticize my plan or argue. She only sighed and I prayed it was out of mercy because maybe she could hear the calamity brewing underneath my tone. Adrian gave me a letter as I left, which basically answered the question I'd asked him when he'd come into my room that second drunken night, "What do you want from me?"

The letter detailed how insecure he'd felt about his intellect growing up, how afraid he was of being attracted to men, and how I had helped him liberate himself. He only wanted me to be happy. Did Adrian or Colt even know what made me happy? Did I even have a clear idea of it myself and if so, did I even have the courage to say it out loud?

In California, I saw the Pacific Ocean for the first time on a warm evening. I went to Urban Outfitters, didn't care for the first time that I was another Black boy that could be arrested, and dumped out my stolen socks in the car. I ate too many edibles in San Francisco before blacking out for an entire day. Disappearing for a while didn't feel so bad. Most of the things I'd learned to love that summer had disappeared too.

Cleveland, Ohio, United States, 2003

The motorcade of cars blocked us on the road during morning traffic. My mother peered into the rearview mirror, straightened her blouse, and then looked at my brother and me in the back seat. Still sleepy eyed, we stared back at her as she hissed, "Don't move. Don't say anything."

The cars turned on their hazards. Then a blond man exited one of them. He was white, wearing a dark-blue suit, and the kind of sunglasses that high schoolers in '80s movies wore. He walked to the driver's-side door and waited for my mother to roll down the window a few inches. He tried to appear as if he wasn't speaking through the window's opening.

"I'm sorry, ma'am. I'm an agent with the FBI and we need to escort you back to your home, your kids included."

My brother, three years older than me and now thirteen years old, simply crossed his arms in the back seat. My heart started to race. Could the FBI have possibly known about little Black kids like me that wanted to be spies? Were they here to snatch me up and train me?

My mother responded tightly, "My kids have school. You wanna make them late for that?"

"It's just protocol. Please allow us to escort you home."

The motorcade escorted us back to our home. We were made to stand in the driveway as the agents roamed and searched our house. The blond man stared at my mother. I wondered if we would all be separated and then interrogated in the black vans that had blocked us on the road. Although I'd read many books about how spies sometimes resorted to torture, they never mentioned *how* they tortured people.

"Have any of you ever seen this man?"

He flashed a photo of a dark-skinned man in his forties. We all shook our heads.

"We've been watching your family for a few weeks because we have reason to believe that you're involved in housing this person. Would there be any truth to that?"

"Truth to the fact that you've been watching my family or that we're housing the man in that photo?"

My mother and the blond man shot lasers at each other with their eyes.

"I've never seen that man before. I have no idea who he is," she added.

The blond man nodded, then prepared to turn. I tugged on his sleeve before my mother could dig her nails into my arm. He looked like a tower as I spoke to him.

"I read a lot of books about spies," I started. "And I wanna learn about tactical surveillance. You be watching us from the rooftops or you rented a place on this street?"

The man blushed, if not for my inquiry, but also because of my mother's burning gaze.

"Maybe one day you'll be a part of the FBI. Just listen to

your mom and stay in school. My agent friends say you have a cleaner room than your brother."

My brother kissed his teeth and crossed his arms as I smiled. The agents left with no evidence or traces of the man in the photo. My mother drove us to school.

■ ■ ■

As a child, my mother got my brother and me to behave in school by telling us that she was omnipotent. She drove us to school, parked outside, and stared at my brother and me before saying, "You better be good in there. If you're not, I'll be watching you through the windows. I'll know."

For years, I peered through the school windows and searched for my mother's thin frame poking out of the bushes. My mother always shrugged confidently when I asked why I hadn't seen her there. Eventually, I realized she couldn't work and set up a lawn chair to watch us with the other parents. Parents were allowed to mythologize themselves to meet the task of looking over us, being the voice in our heads, and ultimately becoming our heroes. This truth was tenfold for immigrant parents, who wanted so desperately for their kids to succeed beyond them. The easiest avenue for success was school.

This seriousness around grades led my brother and I to develop the first of our rituals growing up. On progress report day, he and I congregated outside of the school's front doors with other students milling around us. We opened our envelopes and sighed with relief or exasperation. On the day of my first bad progress report, my hands shook as I stared at the letters on the page. My brother patted me on the shoulder and said the obvious, "You know you can't cry when she finds out, right?" If both of us had gotten bad grades, then the ride back to our house turned into a collective walk up to the guillotine, where we hoped our neighbors would step in and beg for mercy on our behalf.

When it came time to confess our grades, we could be made to stand, to face interrogation, and to grab a leather belt from the cobwebbed treadmill, which would be used to pelt us on the hands. Through the stinging swats of pain in our palms, we were made to explain our academic recklessness, to specify our mistakes, to show our sobbing remorse for failing our most sacred job other than staying out of jail.

My brother and I could rarely buffer the potency of my mother's indignation. Even at that age, I could sense that her rage, when we forgot to do the dishes or broke a figurine in the house or when something went missing, was justified. Women carried the largest percentage of the burden of caring for the young. This was something that seemed wholly natural in my family of caregiving lionesses and wayward lions.

This dynamic made Dennis's entrance into our lives an almost magical occurrence. My new stepfather, Dennis, was a Jamaican man with dark skin and strong arms. He had a penchant for gold jewelry and newsboy hats, and wore a pager on his waist. He thanked my mother when she cooked and smiled at us at the dinner table. My brother, mother, and I often chuckled in secret at how bad of a cook he was, one time producing a brown and unrecognizable soup that sent us running out of the kitchen.

After dinner and a few beers, sometimes Dennis and our mother turned up the stereo's volume, listened to soul music, and swayed together, happy on food and drink and love. My brother groaned as we peered at them from around a corner, but I smiled because that image of them gave me something to believe in.

Even Dennis carried an air of mysticism. As early as I can remember, I loved it when he plopped me on his lap and told me the story of his birth. As he did so, the sunlight reflected the ocean waves in his eyes.

"My mother was with a sailor and had me on a ship. I belong to every country," he'd mutter.

My mother liked to tell me while growing up that I warmed up to Dennis almost immediately after returning to the States from my year in Jamaica. She said, "You seem like you wanted a male role model in your life."

On Sundays, I tagged along with him on long truck rides. With the windows rolled down and "Ain't No Sunshine" blaring, we visited his various friends in Cleveland. I felt proud to be invited into this part of his life, where he gave dap to other Black men in living rooms or debated about the best way to fix a friend's car. He was respected. He was smart and strong. He was a kind man, a vision of what I wanted to be.

■ ■ ■

I don't recall anyone every explaining the FBI searching our home to me. My brother, being older than me, may have received some kind of explanation. Of the two of us, he was already more stoic as the brooding teenager of the house. I still took the general silence from the adults around me as instruction to not be curious even though I hadn't been explicitly told to do so. For the time being, whispers behind closed doors and eavesdropping on phone conversations on my way down the stairs would suffice. Sneaking around to learn more utilized my fascination with detectives, spies, and secret agents. I just wasn't ready to recognize that I was living in the shadows as well.

During the September when I was ten years old, another red flag arose. Aunts and cousins came to our house carrying pots of curry goat, vegetables, rice, and drinks. By five p.m., my mother and her cousins were bumping to Dennis Brown under the glittery plastic chandelier in our dining room. Dennis was in the basement with the other uncles watching football on television. I waited on another couch for all of them to fall asleep. When they never did, I slinked upstairs where my brother and his stepbrother played *Mortal Kombat* on the Nintendo 64. They never let me win. Next I wandered and found my younger cousin, Brandon, hobbling around and trying to drink from other people's cups on tables. When my mother took the stewed chicken out of the oven, everyone clapped until a series of loud knocks rattled our side door.

Everyone froze, waited, and listened.

"It's the Cleveland Police. We got a call from this residence. We're following up. Whoever is inside, open the door now."

Everyone moved like football players completing a drill. Brandon's mother rushed out of the room to find him. Dennis scaled up the stairs from the basement and to the second floor. I looked at my mother, expecting her to return my gaze and give some kind of guidance on where I should place my body during the chaos. Instead she moved toward the door while staring all of the adults down.

As it turned out, Brandon had just learned to call 911. His toddler brain found joy in calling the number whenever he got his hands on a house phone. Ten minutes after the police left, without searching our home, Dennis climbed down from upstairs. My mother handed him a beer. Everyone breathed a temporary sigh of relief.

■ ■ ■

After the FBI raid of our home, Dennis started going on long trips as a truck driver, which sometimes lasted for weeks. By the time I was in sixth grade, my mother instructed me and my brother to start calling him "Uncle Joseph" on the phone and not to mention to our classmates that we had a father living with us. If I asked why, my mother's typical response was, "It's grown-up business. You stick to grades and school and get your degree."

My journal was helping me learn that my family's equation of happiness might not equate to my own. There were things in our home that didn't always sit right with me, like how our home revolved around Dennis. When he returned from a long trip away, he peeled off his boots and sat in his usual spot on the basement sofa. Meanwhile my mother would be cooking, telling me which ingredients to hand her from the cupboards or when to give Dennis a drink refill. Then the dining room table was set and a prayer said, and we'd all eat as a family.

In some ways, I didn't mind. Dennis was warm and kind and deserving of such affection, but it was also apparent that he was being treated this way simply because he was a man. No matter how much the reality was dressed up, I still knew that our beautiful Black family had cracks that these theatrics were trying to cover up.

I could appreciate the life that America was affording our family, but even in middle school, I could already feel myself floating away, changing. After winning my school's spelling bee, I studied for months in preparation for the regional competition. I gathered books from the library on word etymology, studied word lists from the internet, and tried different methods of memorization. When the day came for the regional bee, my English teacher's blue car pulled up to my house. My teacher, a white woman, greeted me warmly. We drove thirty minutes to the auditorium. Sweating and wishing that I had more than just my teacher with me, I walked up to the microphone during the second round and stared out at the audience as the host said my word aloud.

"Presipous?" I repeated, hands sweating as I gripped the microphone and spelled the word. The bell rang and I sauntered offstage as she spelled out the correct version—precipice. My English teacher drove me home before halftime, sprinkling praises on the way as I brooded.

My mother, busy with work and bills, didn't have time to grasp that the experience had rocked me—arriving at the auditorium in a suburb and feeling like Akeelah from *Akeelah and the Bee* as I stared out at all the white faces. Then the humiliation of losing and no one in my family being aware enough to pry about how I had done. It was hard to distinguish if I wanted to be seen and supported, told the truth and left alone, or have a family with the capacity to help me navigate failure.

By the time I was in eighth grade, the popular boys teaching me how to pick up girls started the practical joke of pretending "to be gay for each other." During mass, they'd dry hump each other while cackling in the altar's side room. Sometimes they'd choke each other out in the bathroom.

During the summer after eighth grade, I attended the last of a three-summer-long academic program called the Reach Program. I attended the program's graduation with a sigh of relief after my two previous summers of being taunted by my program peers. I arrived at the University School's auditorium with the twenty-nine other boys, all glistening in our starched clothes. After hors d'oeuvres, our parents took their seats and we took the stage. I sweated under the blaring lights as we did mechanical dance moves to Michael Jackson's "Man in the Mirror." Plastering a smile onto my face and waving my hands was a part of love too; so was knowing which parts of yourself to tuck away to make life easier for other people.

I was a thirteen-year-old puppet on massive, shit-stained strings.

■ ■ ■

We wiped at our faces with rags and climbed the stairs of the rickety apartment building. Ten minutes before, Dennis parked his car across the street from the apartment complex and walked us in. The hallways were dusty and smelled of piss. The dry wall flaked. Some of the windows in the stairwell were broken. Through some of the open apartment doors, I saw older Black men slumped on couches as they watched television. I didn't need to wonder why my mother had never introduced my brother and me to this particular side of the city. Things that looked like the poverty of her upbringing was something worth shielding us from.

"I'm doing for you what I wish someone had done for me growing up," were some of the earliest words I could remember her saying as she buckled me into my car seat as a toddler.

We reached a door. Dennis took a key out of his pocket, then unlocked it. Inside was the bare skeleton of a one-bedroom apartment. Dennis strutted in and opened the windows. Dust fluttered around us.

"Nice, right?"

My mother glanced at him for a moment with her arms still crossed and then shifted her gaze slowly across the space. Something beyond us moved through her eyes. She sauntered over to the bathroom with a sigh as I trailed slowly behind her. She checked the water pressure of the sink, then froze. Her eyes went large. She shrieked.

"What?" my father poked his head inside the bathroom from behind me. "A rat?"

My mother looked to him. He laughed. She rolled her eyes.

For an entire weekend, we wiped the walls and floors, dusted the spiderwebs away, cleaned the windows, and then purified everything with a layer of bleach. Sweat clung to us under the spring heat as we carried the couch up the stairs and into the living room. I marveled at the room. Then, with a pinch of worry, I tried to bridge the distance between our home and this one. Was this meant to be ours or only Dennis's?

My father patted my shoulder and seemed to read my mind. He said, "It's kind of like the tree house you always wanted, huh?"

My mother reiterated to my brother and me in a grave tone that we were prohibited from telling anyone about the apartment. Dennis needed it for privacy.

I only went to the apartment a few times. On one of my visits, I sat in front of the brown TV and flipped through channels. I begged Dennis to buy pizza. I changed the channel to the Miss America competition as soon as he left. For an hour, I watched the slender and poised women wear gowns, bathing suits, and athletic wear. A ritual with bright lights and a celebratory mood always spoke to me. I was hooked by the glamour the audiences and the host washed the women in. An entire world swirled around inside of me, beating against the cage, and tried to get out.

Cleveland, Ohio, United States, 2005–2014

During the winter months when I was eleven, I started crouching in front of the heating vent in my room to read. I got to know Anne Frank while sitting in that spot and reading her diary. The photo on the book's cover showed Anne Frank beaming at the camera, which I always loved. The more I read, the more I felt that I was right there with her as she packed her things away, went into hiding with her family, and essentially did whatever was necessary to grapple with the antisemitism overtaking the world around her.

Her aspirations planted a seed deep inside of me. In one entry she wrote, "I want to go on living even after my death! And therefore I am grateful to God for this gift, this possibility of developing myself and of writing, of expressing all that is in me. I can shake off everything if I write; my sorrows disappear; my courage is reborn. But, and that is the great question, will I ever be able to write anything great, will I ever become a journalist or a writer?"

If writing could help her, a teenage girl trapped in a hiding space in Amsterdam who was also trying to understand her family, then it could help me, a Black boy trying to do the same. Anne's diary was red plaid and had a button to close it. My journal had a heavy wooden cover and an elastic cord to keep it closed. It became my confidant.

When I read her entries about Peter, my stomach flipped every time she described her desire. Anne wanted to be beautiful, brazen, argumentative, seen, and ultimately loved. She described Peter as "tall, slim, and good looking with a serious, quiet, and intelligent face." Anne found a way to love even while locked in her tower, a sort of wounded freedom that could only be manifested by the kind of pressure that made pearls from oysters. My mind wandered to the many times that I snuck into Aunt Vick's bedroom to watch her VHS copy of *Titanic*. I fawned over Jack as he spoke exuberantly about art and life or as he stared at Rose during golden hour. I wondered if I would ever be loved or looked at that way.

I lived in a household where we were meant to report on things that had happened that day at school and encouraged not to hide anything from my parents. I was beginning to learn that I had thoughts worth protecting.

The more I thought about Peter and Jack, the more I thought about how puberty was warping my body in ways that I never expected and the more I felt like I needed to write through the changes. Soft patches of hair grew under my chin. I was taller and suddenly, I couldn't stop glancing at the boy in my seventh-grade class during lessons. Deon was boisterous, athletic, charismatic, and everything that I wasn't.

Deon liked to touch himself during class and wink in my direction jokingly. He was considered the most devastating catch by the girls. Deon watched from afar or simply never noticed when our peers were teasing me. He was also nice enough to chat with me sometimes during class, possibly a symptom of him clocking me as nonthreatening. Even at twelve, I was already aware that there were some things that I wouldn't be in life, being smart and popular included. Navigating both, in my mind, required a degree of slyness and performativity that I didn't possess.

Through all of the changes, I read more voraciously while propped in front of my room's heating vent. With Dennis gone, the house took on a ghostlike quality. My books became a way of battling or confronting these ghosts.

In *Dear Mr. Henshaw*, eleven-year-old middle schooler Leigh Botts becomes pen pals with his favorite writer while his parents went through a divorce. In one letter, Leigh penned, "Sometimes I lie awake listening to the gas station pinging, and I worry because something might happen to Mom. She is so little compared to most moms, and she works so hard. I don't think Dad is that much interested in me. He didn't phone when he said he would."

In *How to Disappear Completely and Never Be Found*, a middle school girl runs away from home to find out the truth about her father's death. The book reads like film noir and ends with an explosive, almost ridiculous realization that her father may have faked his death to hide the fact that he was a werewolf. The night that I finished *Walk Two Moons* by Sharon Creech, I stayed up late and returned to my favorite passages: Salamanca Tree Hiddle reading poetry in front of her class, rushing to the hospital as a cute boy sucks the snake venom out of her grandmother's bite, and staring down into twisted remnants of her dead mother's car wreck while standing on a roadside.

Through these books, I learned the honor of asking questions and seeking answers for the gaping holes in life. Death, or unexplained loss, was often the biggest catalyst for curiosity in the young mind.

"They say that time heals all wounds, but I don't know if they'll heal this one. I just have so much hate in my heart for whoever did this," said my mother while she, Dennis, my brother, and I sat at a restaurant booth. It was spring of 2006 and her brothers, Senel and Derrick, were only murdered two weeks before. She returned from Jamaica with a VHS of their funeral. Grief followed her like a duppy trying to steal my mother.

By the winter of that same year, we had another loss to contend with. I was thirteen when one of Dennis's other sons knocked on our door and told my mother that Dennis had been arrested. My brother and I sat in our parents' bed as our mother told us the news. My mother, the master of fate, appeared helpless. I buried my face in my hands. My brother and mother sat silently until I lifted my face, then my mother asked, "Why are you crying?"

I wanted to run to the bathroom and vomit instead of answering her question. I was witnessing the disintegration of my family (and of the truth) just as my life was meant to start. In all my despair, I realized that I couldn't visualize the last time I had seen Dennis. Was it when my brother and I struggled to clear the driveway of snow so he could leave? Did his gold tooth glint as he smiled and waved? Should we have stopped him from leaving?

More importantly, I couldn't remember how it had felt when I'd seen him.

One night shortly after we found out Dennis had been arrested, my mother handed each of us trash bags.

"We have one hour," she said. "We have to pack up as many of his things as possible and move them."

I held on to the bag, looked at my brother, and then my mother. Our house was dim, so the darkness played at their faces. The entire world was contorting, folding in on itself. Room by room, we gathered as many of his things as possible. We stuffed khaki pants, gold jewelry, sneakers, and more into bags. I stowed away two of his shirts to have when I missed him, hoping that my mother would never find them and be angry. We drove to our cousins' house and hid the contents in their garage. Staring at the garage while standing under the moonlight, my brother asked why we had to hide his things.

My mother replied, "It has to be like he was never here."

I wanted more than the scavenged shirts that I had saved. I wanted the winter Sundays when he watched football and my mother handed me mugs of hot chocolate. I wanted the long summer drives down to Florida, where I could stand next to Dennis on the beach as he squeezed my shoulder. The clearing away of him felt forced and mystic. It was also a clearing away of the illusion of our normal family. His imprisonment was one layer of cement encasing this new world. All of our family's coping mechanisms were the other layers. There was no space, imagination, or time for me to bust open the door of his eastside apartment with a crowbar, find him sitting on the musty couch, and have a conversation with him about how quickly things were changing. The change was here—the Jamaican child born wayward on a boat now consumed by the belly of America.

Winter turned to spring, but the passing weeks brought no reassurance. My brother and I were still prohibited from telling any of our classmates about our father's arrest. I continued to eavesdrop on phone calls and casually ask my brother questions about what was going on. It was only through this method that I learned that Dennis had been living with us illegally after being deported back to Jamaica years before, that the police were attempting to pin him with trumped-up drug-dealing charges. My brain short-circuited. I couldn't distinguish if what I was feeling was heartbreak, shame, or a mixture of both. I knew that I wanted things to be like they were before. I also knew that that was impossible.

I wrote in my journal about how it became our jobs to turn Dennis into a ghost, something that appears in a dream and fades away as soon as you begin to open your eyes. I used my laptop to start researching some of the feelings that I was having, especially toward other boys in my grade. The more I searched, the more I found a world of teenagers online either afraid or all too ready to speak their truths.

I looked up gay porn online, tried to rewire my brain by forcing myself to watch straight porn after and attempted to read the Bible from start to finish in the sixth grade. The more I stared at the words, went to school, was mistreated by my classmates, and saw how teachers evaded pointed questions about God, the more confused I became. I thought of all the Sunday services that I'd attended as I stared around at all the Black bodies jumping up in exuberance. Women flung their hats from their heads. Their feet stomped furiously at the ground. Others cried and kneeled at the altar. The preacher always called people in need of guidance to the front. My grandma nudged Princess and me toward the fervor every once in a while. The churchgoers descended and rested their hands on our shoulders, speaking in tongues. I felt the weight of their faith, then and now.

As we walked away from the church, I'd asked Princess, "Did you feel anything?"

"I think it takes time to feel something. Sometimes I do."

I tried to embody this logic through all of my religious due diligence. I believed in God as a means to dismantle the disease inside of me. Even after praying and crying myself to sleep as I thought of the years ahead, I still awoke with the same sensation in my gut. The chaos inside of me was being unleashed onto the world, but I didn't want to destroy any more of my life and my world before it even began.

Following Dennis's arrest, our house was robbed. Closets were opened. Drawers and dressers were overturned. Clothes were flung off the racks and all our gifts were stolen. Someone real and alive had come to take our things. In my mind, the robbery was some manufactured plan from the universe trying to search for the man that we had erased. In order to earn an insurance payout for the robbery, we called the police to get a report. After the police left, my mother came into the dining room and revealed, "Your father is upset. Said he cried in his jail cell because he couldn't help us."

Sundays were no longer for church visits or family dinners. Instead we sometimes showered, ate a heavy breakfast, and drove to the sterile gray building in Youngstown, Ohio.

Past the barbed wire, the ringing doors, and metal detectors was the waiting room. I learned to empty out all of my pockets quickly and hold my head high under the gaze of the mostly white prison staff. Sometimes as I walked by, I glared at them and wondered if they noticed that most of the prisoners were Black, brown, or poor. What did it feel like to be a captor or a part of a history repeating itself?

The visits were not the time to be brutally honest with Dennis in the way that I wanted to be. I desired time alone with him to begin to tell him some of the feelings that I was having, the arguments at home with my mother, and the prospect of high school around the corner. Instead, my mother and Dennis embraced. He clapped his hand on my brother's and my shoulders. We performed stories of our most recent life updates. We were puppets on strings as the cameras in all corners watched.

■ ■ ■

If I couldn't trust the adults in my life, maybe I could learn to trust myself. I came home to an empty house again because my mother and brother were both at work. On *The Oprah Winfrey Show*, Oprah talked to a friend, who was a gay man. They joked about what it would take for him to have sex with a woman, and then Oprah said, "It makes no sense to me that you should hate yourself. Just let it go. Be whoever you are meant to be."

It haunted me that when Oprah spoke, her expression was not tinged with disgust that many of the adults I knew had for gay people. She looked at me, the viewer, with a parental love and protectiveness that I craved. I broke. The disease festering inside of me shriveled up. Even though I was terrified, I turned to my journal with shaky hands and a dry throat. I wrote the truth for the first time in code, "9. 1, 13. 7, 1, 25." I eventually found the courage to write, "I am gay and this is going to explode my world." I realized that choosing to love myself was not the paramount decision. The crux was how committed to self-love I was, how I defined it, and how I defended it.

With this realization, writing became the elixir to many of my mental wounds. I sat at my desk as my pregnant eighth-grade teacher turned to the class and brushed her black hair behind her ear.

"I want you all to write a short story about whatever you want. Anything at all, just make it three to five pages," she said.

Everyone cleared their desks and packed up to go home. I was slow to leave as my mind raced with all of the possibilities. I went home, sat at my desk cluttered with piles of R. L. Stine books, and hunched over my laptop. If life was breaking down all around me, at least I could use my mind to build something. That evening I turned into my own God, one that was capable of giving redemption.

My teacher called me into her classroom during recess after I turned in the short story. This teacher was far from my favorite. A few weeks before I'd told her that I had problems with the other boys in my grade being mean to me, which was an understatement. She replied, "Maybe if you didn't act differently, then they wouldn't treat you differently."

"Now, Prince. I read your short story and I can tell that you put so much work into it," she said. "But I'm concerned about why you wrote it."

She handed the story back to me marked with an A and folded her hands in front of her at her desk. I tried to wrap my head around what she was saying, or better yet, asking.

"I just thought it would be a cool story," I replied.

"How are things at home?"

I detected a sort of knowing and unknowing in her gaze and was confused. If children being hurt mattered to adults, especially Black adults, wouldn't they be more keen on not whipping their children or blaming them for being bullied?

"I don't know what you're really asking, but things are fine at home. My mom and dad are both working. We're fine."

"And she doesn't hurt you, like the boy in this story was hurt?"

In my story, a boy comes home from school with his best friend to find his mother in a drunken rage. An argument ensues between the boy and his mother. She grabs a knife and stabs him. When he wakes up in the hospital, he is asked to testify against his mother in court so that his father, who is loving, can get custody of him. After giving a witness testimony, the main character leaves the court to a mob of reporters while holding his father's hand.

I left school that day and tried to interrogate why I'd written such a thing and why the prospect of it excited me. Those three pages hadn't been enough to explore the emotional life of the main character. The more I thought, the more I realized why I'd written it. I hoped that some part of me could do the same thing as my story's character when the time came. I wanted to have the courage to turn the steering wheel and change the route of what was to come.

I wrote stories about teenagers being flung midair during car accidents, avenging their parents' murders, being kidnapped, exposing terrorist plots, fleeing slashers during high school dances, and having love affairs. These stories provided light during the dim months of teenagedom, but they didn't totally help me unearth myself. If I stared out at the world of those early stories, they mimicked me staring out at the auditorium during that regional spelling bee. There were lots of white middle-class teenagers looking for meaning in a world that could challenge them, but usually catered to them. I wasn't aware of what I was expressing because the earliest messages I'd been fed were to perform well, put on a good face, and infiltrate the white world to give back to my people.

But what was I to do if my people didn't even understand me?

I became editor of my middle school's newspaper and started to feel more confident in my writing. I shared new writings with my mother. After peeling her boots off after work one day, cooking dinner, and corralling us to do our homework, she sat with me at the kitchen table and I handed her the newest pages of my short story. She glanced at them and then handed them back to me.

"I'm too tired right now. I'll read them later."

I couldn't argue because I empathized with her fatigue. I never took offense at her lack of enthusiasm. By that point, writing had become my own. It was a marker of the kind of person that I was or a grappling for something that could differentiate me from my peers. I craved this kind of definitiveness.

During all of my writings and readings, I wished my teachers would have introduced me to the class of subversive

Black men that had once lived and what they meant to Black culture. I didn't yet know about James Baldwin moving to Paris, drinking into the late-night hours as he battled his guilt about leaving America and the ghost of his best friend, Eugene Worth. If I had, I would have learned that the dead can always come back through the work of those that they loved. I didn't know about Black men like Malcolm X or the complexity that they held. Men who went to prison, became radicalized, and left with a zeal to change the world. Or Essex Hemphill, a dark-skinned poet living with HIV that stared back at the camera with a knowing of what it meant to live a full life. In my writing, I was grasping at straws and trying to live in the body of the "white other." I was trying to escape a body that I was afraid would eventually engulf everything around me in flames when it exploded.

By the age of fifteen, I'd written my first three novels. I felt holy sitting in front of my laptop for hours on end while envisioning full worlds. Every character had a missing father or some form of sexual confusion. Even if they were white, I couldn't write them without unpacking my own problems.

■■■

High school meant that I was a new victim to bullying. A girl called me a faggot in front of the class on the first day. If I left lunch early, I could fall prey to the group of third years that liked to push me into lockers. I met Nadia at the end of a tumultuous freshman year. The next year, we were seated next to each other in a social studies class and quickly descended into whispered jokes. She was medium height, brown skinned, and had big boobs and an airy temperament that I loved.

"You were so damn quiet when I met you," she recalled once, "I thought you didn't even know how to talk."

The wall that I'd built between myself and others was lifting. Nadia and our group of nerdy, indie music–obsessed friends were the reason. It was only months into our friendship when I started to tire of pretending that I was straight. Antoinette, another friend in the group with an incarcerated father was openly bisexual, and I admired her for it. On one of our many after-school phone calls, Nadia and I talked about crushes.

"You know what? I could imagine you being with a boy one day," she said.

I sat up a little more in my chair. I cleared my throat. The room was hot.

"I think I could too."

Nadia took the news well, becoming the first person I felt like I could wholly confide in. Through this and more, we became fused. She giggled with me as I made a profile on Trevorspace, a social network for queer teens. The internet helped me compare experiences with other gay teens and even prompted me to try to date. Since my mother had met Nadia's parents, she was fine with me casually hanging out at Nadia's house. Everyone in my family assumed that Nadia and I were dating. I mostly loved how warm and comedic her family was.

Nadia's father was a former chef and cooked a mean seafood pasta. Her mother, Crystal, was encouraging, witty, and tried to wrangle in Nadia's light-hearted disposition. I liked to tell her that she was smart and amounted to more than the stares at her chest by the other boys in our high school. Nadia, in turn, gave me a Black family that could accept me for who I was—a gay boy terrified of what was to come.

The feared moment arrived when my mother tore through my room, read my journal, and shook me awake afterward to ask if I was gay. In those early morning hours, I watched her cry.

"You must have been hurt by someone. Someone must have touched you. Nobody touch you too when you were little, did they? You have too many friends that are girls. You should have played sports more. Who is putting these ideas in your head? Don't you know that this is sick?"

While she showered, I tore the journal into a thousand pieces and tossed them into the trash outside. I went to school and cried to my friends at my locker until my head pounded. I was running through a wall of flames and there was no one that could offer me water. The handful of gay people that I knew had yet to come out to their parents. Two weeks after the conversation with my mother and Aunt Vick, she took me to another parking lot. It was early summer. I didn't have the daily distractions of seeing my friends at school.

"I'm going to have you meet a friend of mine," was all she said before opening her door and instructing me to exit the car as well.

My mother had started reading the Bible more voraciously, even sitting me down on one occasion to quote applicable verses about why my "condition" was a sin. Her disapproval didn't cloud everything, but it was still a thorn caught in my side.

"I'm Gloria," said the woman who got out of the car next to us and held out her hand.

I eyed her. She was in her forties with a butch haircut. She wore loose-fitting pants and a blouse. Gloria had a warm enough air about her, but I was used to feigning recognition with adults that knew my mother, a hairdresser that had many clients after decades of work. I didn't want to be rude, so I shook Gloria's hand.

"I'm gonna drive you around and talk to you about some of the problems you've been having," she said. "Is that alright?"

I shoved my hands into my hoodie pockets and tried to stop my shoulders from sinking. I looked at my mother and she stared back blankly. Did I have enough time to text Nadia to tell her where I was? As I climbed into the woman's car, I memorized her license plate number. Gloria took me to a local park, stopped her car, and gazed ahead.

"It's a beautiful day, isn't it?"

"Yeah," I replied shortly.

"I don't want you to be alarmed because of how strange this might seem to you. I'm your mother's friend. I've known her for quite a few years. She's done my hair. She's considering going to my church."

"That's great," I muttered with the enthusiasm of a dying mule.

Gloria sighed. I rolled down my window. I noticed that she hadn't locked the car doors. I decided that it would be too alarming if I got out my phone to text.

"Do you feel like you have a problem? You can be honest with me, if you want. I used to be like you."

I looked at her more directly and recognized something in her eyes. A sadness that forced me to level with her, if only a little. I couldn't help that it softened me.

161

"What do you mean that you used to be like me?"

"I was attracted to women in my twenties," she forced a laugh as she spoke. "I was wild. It was the '80s. Everything was all over the place. I'd go out to clubs, drink, and be with all kinds of women. I scared the shit out of my mother."

Gloria unraveled her history of battling her feelings toward other women, the subsequent fall out with her mother, and how they became estranged. She talked about how her "lifestyle" led to her mother having a heart attack. She cried, which felt like a manufactured desperation to me. I wondered how many other teenagers she had told this story to.

"Are you prepared to have this hurt your mother and family?"

It was a hard question. I thought for a few moments before I answered. I could only be honest.

"It's not something that I can bow out of. I've already tried being unhappy by going against it. I can't let people tell me who I am. I've had a lot of people do it. Eventually, I looked at myself and wondered why I hated what I saw looking back at me so much."

I didn't tell her about the pornography that I'd found on the computer of two Black men making love when I was eight years old, and how I'd known that it wasn't my mother or my stepfather who had been watching it. I didn't tell her how I'd been a bully and called a boy a faggot with my friends. I didn't tell her about how my mother sometimes looked at me like I was someone that she didn't even know. These were all things that I'd learned that adults didn't want to hear about or really confront.

"But isn't that a selfish choice? Where does God lie for you?"

Now I started to get angry, so I turned it right around at her.

"If my family makes me hate myself and I kill myself, whose hands is the blood on? Where is God then? There are people in Jamaica that get killed because they like men or they like women or they're transgender. Where is their God? Who saves them?"

Gloria's eyes cut away. She looked out the front window, so I did the same. Fathers walked by while pushing strollers. I felt a pressure building behind my eyes as I wished that I could just go back to being the little kid in Jamaica running around in my grandmother's yard.

"I was able to change because I chose to believe that God had a bigger plan for me, a more holy plan. I want the same for you."

"How can you help if you don't know me?" I replied. "I'm sorry that all those bad things happened, but we're not the same. What if it's loyalty, not love, that your mother wants?"

Gloria took me back to the restaurant parking lot. For the rest of the day, I couldn't look at my mother. The conversation with Gloria had dragged some hidden part of me out that I'd been protecting from this fucked-up storm. The entire conversation added insult to injury when my mother interrogated me that night about a secret that I'd revealed to Gloria—that I'd told my older brother that I was gay and he hadn't cared at all.

Soon after my mother started going to the same church as Gloria. Somewhat out of guilt and somewhat to appease my mother, I occasionally attended Sunday services with her. Greased in Vaseline, we'd make it to the church in University Circle. The riotous instruments and clapping filled the tall room. Ornate dresses got sweated through as a woman ran through the aisles after kicking off their heels. While the spirit took everyone else, my mother simply sat down with her hands folded in her lap. I waited for a meteorite to flatten us all.

There was always the point in the service after the preacher asked the question for the millionth time. He stood before everyone with his forehead glistening, opened his arms, and spoke.

"Now is the time for those that seek the Lord to step forward. If you are feeling beaten down by life,"—I yawned in my seat in reaction to his words—"know that your Lord and Savior is here to guide you if you accept him into your heart."

This time, it was not a light nudge of a child to the front. My mother placed her hand on my forearm. Hell burned underneath us. I tried to swallow through the dry heat in my throat as she said, "Don't you think you should go up there?"

I forced myself to live through the discomfort of wriggling my arm out of my mother's grip and slipping off to the bathroom to stare at myself in the mirror, to remind myself that I didn't need or want to be saved by anyone because that dream had ended a long time ago. I sometimes ran into Gloria in the hallway with my mother as we left church. She shook my mother's hand, then smiled at me and said hello. I stared back, forcing my expression not to change, and said, "I've gotta go to the car."

In the hot car, I stewed with my thoughts and tried to face the fact that I had compelled my mother to go to church, to find God, to find this woman to manipulate her child, and to ultimately seek refuge from this new calamity, which was me.

If anything at all gave me hope for the near future, it was the news that I was accepted on a scholarship to attend the Kenyon Young Writers Workshop. As I was the avid bibliophile of my grade, my English teacher recommended that I apply. Nadia and I shopped for supplies for my short stay in a dorm room for the first time. My mother threatened that if I had sex while I was away, she could have me checked by a doctor. I resisted the urge to laugh in her face because I knew if I did, she may slap me. I had already come out to my doctor as gay the year before. Instead of the ridicule I feared, my doctor, who had known me since I was a baby, looked at me, told me it was going to be okay, and handed me pamphlets on safe sex.

Gambier, Ohio, was a sleepy, small town. During the workshop's long lunches, I walked up and down the Middle Path with my new friend, Candice, a girl whose family was from Africa. Candice had grown up under a domineering father that shaved her head when she started to blossom as a woman.

"His way of punishing me," she explained.

I loved her stillness and laughter immediately. We sat between the bookshelves in the local bookstore while eating ice cream, our legs blocking the aisle. She was the first person I came out to at the workshop. I wanted someone to confide in.

"I don't know how to tell these people that I'm gay. It's terrifying," I said to her. I didn't think I could handle more pain.

But there was another gay boy from Cleveland named Jesus at the workshop. On the first day, he spotted me in a lounge area and walked over to me. He was a dancer at an arts school down the street from mine. He held my hand a little longer than normal when he shook it, wore Capri pants and long scarves, and had hair dyed wild colors. We bonded over being scholarship kids, growing up in Cleveland, being gay, and having fathers in prison. His gaze made me sweat, not because I was attracted to him, but because a boy had never had a crush on me before.

The workshop was my first time really socializing with white people. For days, I didn't understand their jokes or why they were funny. They were from cities all around the country that I'd never heard of, and when I asked a boy to trade his sunglasses with me for a book I'd just bought, he laughed.

"These are Ray Bans. I can't trade these for a book."

At the workshop, it was not hard to make friends. I liked the nerdy undertone of even the cool kids and found myself in kinship with the more comical crowd. The workshop aligned with my birthday, so everyone sang to me during lunch. Jesus brought me a cupcake with a candle in it. My friends who I hadn't come out to nudged me and teased that they thought Jesus had a crush on me. I scoffed and tried to make some sly joke.

Every morning I woke up, showered, left my dorm room, and attended three workshops a day. By the end, my three-subject notebook was nearly filled. I wrote my first piece of fiction about two boys from different worlds that fall for each other. I wrote up a response to a prompt, and the story I detailed had the entire room laughing. I had never moved people in such a way with my writing. For the first time in my life, I felt like a writer.

Life was propelling me toward wanting to hold on to the very thing, writing, that had outed me to my mother. I still felt my therapist's words when she told me, "No matter what happens now or how your family treats you, you still have to decide who you want to be. This is not forever."

The answer had been in front of me the entire time. Words could be the plywood, nails, and sails that sent me off into a world of my own making. A few months later, I finished writing another novel. By fall of our senior year, Nadia and I sat at her dining room table while applying for college. I decided that I would be an English major.

I went to prom and didn't tell anyone that I kept my biological father's photograph in my pocket or that I decided on the university that I was going to. As my friends and I swayed on the dance floor and as my stepfather was being released from prison, then sent back to Jamaica in the spring of my senior year in 2011, an undeniable part of me was ready for the future. I only had one more dragon to slay on my journey there.

■ ■ ■

That summer, my brother and I stayed with Dennis in Kingston, where he now lived. We ate cereal with watered-down condensed milk. We went to the beach and smiled at each other over dinner. I tried to prepare myself.

I sat my father down in my room during my last week in Kingston and asked him what I'd been wondering since he'd been away.

"Would you care if I was gay?"

Dennis shifted where he sat, got up, and closed the door. He looked at me again. He had more gray hairs on his head than I remembered. He'd lost a lot of weight while away. Whenever there was a breeze, I liked to look at him as he breathed in deep. I wondered how much he had wanted to do that while he'd been locked up. The whole thing felt like a race we'd been running together. Now I couldn't tell if he had stopped or if I had. Or maybe the target had changed. I had changed.

"Why would you ask that?"

"Because I'm gay," I said.

There was another long silence, the kind that swallows all the warmth in the room. He sighed, then said, "That's not what God intended . . . Don't tell me someone touched you when you were younger?"

I swallowed my pride and dodged his questions about anal sex, about my thoughts on hell, and even when he told me that he didn't want this part of me to be a part of his life. We walked away from each other, like two soldiers after a narrow battle. The grenade-blast shock left my ears ringing and my insides churning. The whole time, the whole fucking time, I had been made to feel like the destruction was born in me and was now wreaking havoc as it escaped, as it emaciated me. Dennis's reaction and rejection bludgeoned this fallacy to death. It consumed all the glittery memories in his car on hot Saturdays and all the performances I'd done as the "good son" during those jail visits. The veil that I wore and that he loved was now pulled away to reveal my true face.

As he spoke, he couldn't really look me in the eye, and it was only then that I realized it. My parents were the puppets performing for each other, all orchestrated by malevolent strings. I was not.

Before I boarded the plane back to the US, I willed myself to hug him goodbye. On the plane, I took periodic trips to the bathroom. Sitting and staring and thinking made my eyes well up in a matter of moments when I let my mind drift away. In the bathroom, I clutched the sink. I breathed. I tried to release the pain that Dennis had imparted onto me. Even then, I still had hope in the prospect of moving to college and starting a new chapter of my life.

A month later, my mother, my brother, and I moved large boxes to my third-floor dorm room. No longer were we working to hide the evidence of a man.

The heat had subsided a little when my mother sat me down on a bench. Holding my hands, she looked at me and said, "Don't be gay while you're here. Please."

I blinked. I froze. I hugged them both. I watched my mother and brother drive off in their car. The same feeling swirled through my gut when I stood in my high school parking lot, and when I walked away from Dennis in the airport. It was my family releasing me to universe, or more precisely, my last moment to hold on to, something that had already faded away.

■ ■ ■

I made the dean's list my first semester and spent my free time joining LGBTQIA organizations. At the meetings with mostly white gays, I shrugged as they demanded to know how I could be gay if I hadn't seen *Grease* yet. Their coming-out stories didn't sound like the cracked sidewalks on the east side of Cleveland, doing prison visits in high school, or unpacking the influence of colonialism on Jamaican culture. My experiences, no matter how complex, were muddled among their whiteness and self-indulgence. I went to parties and watched as they kissed, drank, danced, and left together.

During the spring break of my sophomore year, I went back to Cleveland. My mother found a video about my coming-out story that I'd posted online. She grabbed my arm, livid, and tried to coax me into the basement alone to talk to her. My mind flashed to the night she learned I was gay by reading my journal and all the horrible things she said afterward. I pulled my arm away, stood firm, and refused to follow her. With my entire world suddenly closing in on me, I called my brother and asked him to pick me up. He came home, listened to my mother berate me, and then said to me, "I used to feel like you do. You just have to grow up."

Even gay brothers can find ways to betray each other.

For all the baggage that I carried with me and hoped to unload as an adult free from the confines of home, I still hadn't found my new chosen family. I wanted more from a queer community than white queer people taking up more space. I watched the documentary *We Were Here* during my junior year. Set moodily in San Francisco during the AIDS epidemic, the film interviewed a group of people that survived. As the film progressed, the viewer dives deeper into the devastation of the virus and the government's apathy as hundreds of thousands of people died nationwide. The film defined the struggles of the San Francisco LGBTQIA community with their own stories and emotion. It compared queer survival in the AIDS epidemic to surviving a kind of war.

The pain in the film flipped a switch in me and I went home to write. What I wrote was a novel called *Stand Alone*. The first line read, "Matthew had expected it to feel different."

Matthew encapsulated all the heavy and traumatized parts of myself from coming out to my parents. His fictional town of

White Gate was a metaphor for my home growing up, which often felt empty and too quiet on evenings after school, especially while my father was in prison. His relations with the sheriff's son, a nearly doomed love affair, was my imagining what it would have been like to fall messily in love in high school. What sort of madness would have ensued then?

Matthew loved his mother despite her coldness, wanted emotional closeness with his brother despite the bitterness born between them, and succumbed to self-hatred after being forced into a conversion therapy program. I had faced my own years of self-hatred in the nights I prayed to God to change me and in the curses I attacked myself with when I became weak at the sight of gay porn.

Once he's sent away to conversion therapy, his facade of stoicism fades when he finds a letter that his mother wrote to a mysterious man before his birth. Matthew sneaks out of his room at night, calls his mother, and pleads her for understanding. When she rejects him, he breaks, is sent to solitary confinement, and eventually is subjected to electroshock therapy. Afterward Matthew goes to a rooftop, stares up at the sky in a haze, and a fellow program member, Grant, tells him, "You let them win, you're handing your life over. Make a choice."

When Matthew and Grant decide to run away, they are two young people attempting to find refuge in each other on the highways of America. Eventually Matthew decides to return to White Gate by hitchhiking. On the journey back, he survives on the kindness of strangers offering him rides, food, and advice. He is reminded that life is not over. He plays soccer with kids on a roadside in Tennessee, talks to teenagers about their lives on their way to a wedding, and stares up at the sky while eating cake in the bed of a pickup truck.

The novel ends in the burnt skeleton of the barn that the two lovers previously frequented. Keith, the sheriff's son, agrees to leave White Gate with Matthew. The last lines of the book read: "As the morning light struck Matthew's face, he knew that White Gate would soon be a distant memory, a traveler in the rearview mirror with his thumb jutting outward, forever waiting for some new place to go."

The novel was a goodbye, a diary, a manifesto, and a promise. I wanted to see Matthew feel pain, wallow in it, confront his demons, and grow bold enough to love someone with intention and choice. I finished *Stand Alone* and looked up at my living room in a blur. I closed my laptop. A choice had been made, only the choice was for me this time.

I realized that all myths and stories are not bad, as long as they bring us and others closer to the truth. Weeks after I finished writing the novel, I called my own mother to ask her why she pushed me away after I came out and told her how much it hurt. On the phone, my mother rejected my pleas and, like Matthew, I cried.

Literature taught me the importance of acknowledging where a question or emotion could take you. Who was my father facing in that car on that day in February 1995? A tree, as beautiful and as life-giving as it could be, still reminded me of his grave, unmarked and under some sycamore tree in a cemetery on a hot summer morning as my flip-flops sunk into the dewy grass. I was beginning to realize that I needed to find where he existed in my world to finally make sense of him.

Where does a Black boy go when he is offered less than his spirit needs? And what does he become? Outlaw, revolutionary, none, or both.

Whatever I became, I would have to start as a traveler on the roadside of America, fading away into oblivion in someone else's rearview mirror.

Big Sky, Montana, and Seattle, Washington, United States; and Paris, France, 2015–2016

For the summer of 2015 after I graduated college, I was a house-keeper at dinky hotel at a ski resort in Big Sky, Montana. While scrubbing toilets and fixing up beds, I listened to speeches by Malcolm X, Kathleen Cleaver, Martin Luther King Jr., and Angela Davis. I marveled at the snap of Malcolm X's jokes, which were good enough for him to lead the laughter on, and wiped bathroom mirrors as Malcolm X's analogy about progress and the knife rang in my ears.

I worked long, lonely hours with a squeaky cart in deserted hallways of the hotel. After work, I smoked weed with my co-workers, who were mostly white self-proclaimed snow birds, and marveled at how small I could feel while working a job that once again controlled my housing, coworkers, friends, and meals. The strange sunken place made certain things tolerable, like my white peers joking about how cool Rachel Dolezal was or risking my life by getting into the back seats of cars with drunken drivers. It didn't seem fair that fun also seemed so entangled with destruction.

One morning during a bus ride to work, I met a white man with a scraggly ponytail. We chatted about the weather. He introduced himself as Wesley and invited me to his dorm for drinks after work. In his room, we drank whiskey out of red Solo cups and I stayed chipper as the conversation wandered to liberals whining about the Confederate flag. I argued weakly with him until Wesley promised that he wasn't racist because he attended the most diverse high school in his county where his best friend was Black.

"Maybe you think he's your friend, but he never really trusted you. Black people don't always tell you the truth," I said and ignored Wesley when he scoffed, took a long sip of whiskey, and went on a tangent about affirmative action.

Only an hour into hanging out, Wesley excused himself to the bathroom. I waited for twenty minutes before checking in on him. Wesley, this forty-something-year-old man, lay sideways in the shower and was sobbing. I couldn't understand his muffles until I got closer and egged him on.

"This country ain't what it used to be," he cried again and again and again.

In that moment, I realized something new as I thought of the love I felt when I heard the vigor in Malcolm X's voice and what it meant for it to be so easy to shoot down a man like him down in front of a crowd of people. No matter what you did, America could fold your story into its own; whether you are the revolutionary that got what was coming to him or the good child told to be kind to others, to hear them out, and to brush it aside when a man double your age tries to get you drunk and defends the very systems that could destroy you.

■ ■ ■

The mayhem of working in Montana made it easy for me to accept a job offer in Seattle. By August of 2015, I left Big Sky and moved my meager belongings to Seattle, Washington. The move warmed my mother, who was eager for her son to turn away from nomadism and toward an expected milestone of adulthood.

My boss at my job as a boycott organizer for a union introduced himself as Kevin. He was a white trans man from the Midwest that seemed keen on proving that he could survive outside of it. His work ethic was the topic of gossip among the organizers. They shook their heads in amazement when I told them that Kevin had me phone-bank for the union a half an hour after helping me move a couch into my new apartment. During a work trip to San Francisco, he pressured another coworker, Emily, and me to work long hours on picket lines. When Emily talked to our bosses about how it was affecting her health, they responded, "When you applied to this job, you should have considered your health conditions."

The lack of say in our hours and our bosses' flippant attitude toward Emily really dug at me. These white union organizers wore a mask of justice while silencing Emily and me. For over a month, I talked to other organizers in the union about our hypocritical work environment. We met at cafes during lunch and spoke in hushed voices. I looked at the other organizers, who were older or had families, and saw the fear in their eyes as they spoke about why it would be difficult to change the problematic things about our job. Although I understood their desire for a stable income to support their families, I couldn't understand how they reconciled their complacency while younger organizers, like me, became burnt out.

White America was doing political gymnastics right in front of my very eyes. I had been nudged into capitalist adulthood, the kind of circus where elephants balance cups of shit on their trunks. With every paycheck that I received, the more a sense of guilt clouded me until I told the truth.

I stood on my apartment's first-floor balcony with a beer in hand as I explained to my mother the long hours, the lack of say in my work environment, and my general unhappiness. There was a long pause. Then she sighed before saying, "This is just what our people do. We work, and it's like I always say. You—"

"You have to kiss ass before you can kick it," I finished for her.

The union job was my first experience with a salary. For my mother, a salary was the ideal landing pad for me, a Black college graduate with an English degree. She didn't understand how I turned my past year of organizing student demonstrations into a job that could cover my rent and bills, and give me enough pocket change to go to the bars. She seemed proud in a way that felt misplaced to me until that conversation on the phone when her anecdote jolted me backward to my bloody lip behind the dumpster at Our Lady of Peace, to the trash bags of Dennis's things crammed into the garage, and to fabled apartment we weren't meant to tell anyone about. I realized it wasn't the battle at hand that I was contending with, but rather, the world that had created the struggle for Black people, young and old, in the first place.

"I get what you're saying, but I think you deserved more when you came to the US. So did grandma. So do I."

"What does better and paying the bills look like?" she asked.

She had me stumped there. I thought of the Black driver throwing his cigarette out the window and of what Aunt Vick said to my mother about my father's death as they stared at my infant body in the hospital. Black people couldn't live without sacrifice. Sacrifice is how we are taught to know we are strong. So it becomes a matter of what we lose with the sacrifices that we do choose.

■ ■ ■

A month later, I was fired from my boycott organizing job after a disciplinary hearing where a union boss told me that the union had to "replicate capitalism within its structure to beat capitalism."

I packed up my things, returned my work phone, and shoved the bottle of vodka that I kept in my desk into my messenger bag. I walked to Pike Place Market and sat at my favorite spot, the chairs past the fish stalls that overlooked the Puget Sound.

I didn't dare call my mother right away to say that I'd been fired. My mind played a memory on loop from my first day at the job. I called a Lyft to work. Once my ride was parked outside of the Seattle Masonic Labor Temple, I stared out the window at the building's tan brick until the driver spoke up.

"You alright, son?"

I cleared my throat and answered, "I'm starting as a paid organizer for a labor union. I moved here a few weeks ago."

He cut off the radio and leaned toward his window.

Later, as a I sat on my barstool at Pike Place Market, the driver's reply before I left his Lyft, rang in my ears: "In my day, we didn't get paid to organize."

I left my barstool, which had a view through massive windows that overlooked the shimmering water, and walked to Left Bank Books. I wandered the shelves that stretched to the ceilings, fingered the zines, and finally settled on my next read—*Revolutionary Suicide* by Huey Newton.

■ ■ ■

In my two-month stint of unemployment, I found it hard to do more than smoke weed, watch *Broad City*, and read Huey Newton's memoir. I liked the idea of Newton hitchhiking through California, reading heavy philosophical texts, and showing up to class drunk. I liked the conversations he had with other Black people in his Oakland apartment over cigarettes and drinks about how campus organizing often differed from changing the lives of "the brothers on the block." This was a notion that I was stumbling into as I filled my gut with cheap booze and tried to navigate the colorblindness of the spaces that I was forcing myself to enjoy.

Once I was done with Newton's memoir, I expanded to other Black writers and immediately became enamored with James Baldwin. He was born in New York City, waited tables in Greenwich Village, fell out of love with the church, and lost his best friend to suicide. Then he fled the United States for Paris in 1948. There was a romance and a tragedy to how he described arriving in Paris with no money, no friends, and a desire to be more.

I watched whatever YouTube videos I could find of interviews that he'd done and learned abut the wave of Black writers that moved abroad. The zeal with which these Black men lived started to haunt me. I used what little money I had to visit Ohio for the holidays and relayed my desires to travel and experience something new to Nadia's father. I went over the itinerary repeatedly until the walls of my brain were raw with the details.

Nadia's father looked at me as we stood in his kitchen on New Year's Eve, smiled, and then said, "You must really trust yourself."

With Nadia at my side, I entered 2016 and decided to be the kind of person that was willing to fall, if not run, toward his dreams. Even though I didn't fully trust myself, Nadia's father's assumption was all that I needed. I packed too many clothes into a duffel bag and filled a backpack with prized books I planned to read during my three weeks away.

I sold my furniture, subleased my room, and told my mother my plans. She reacted with dismay and tears because she had given me a nest egg of money after college to move to Seattle. An investment that had seemingly gone to waste. Her stable son was wayward once more.

But I couldn't get Huey's words out of my head. Huey, who was deemed too small and fought to defend himself against boisterous neighborhood boys, who was scolded by teachers and romped around Oakland, and who only learned how to read because of his older brother, Melvin's, love for poetry. No one knew he would go on to brandish shotguns at police officers from his back seat or become a vision of hope. I believed him when he wrote, "Black men and women who refuse to live under oppression are dangerous to white society because they become symbols of hope to their brothers and sisters, inspiring them to follow their example."

Whatever nameless revolution came my way, I would face it as Huey had and surely as only I could.

***

I roamed the streets of the Paris suburb with my friend's note clutched in my hand. The heat of that spring day and the shaking in my body were months in the making. When I finally found the address on the piece of paper that my friend had handed to me, I thought of her words, "Go here. Meet my friends. Talk to Enzo. You'll have a place to stay."

I knocked and waited. The door flung open. I immediately realized that I didn't even know what Enzo was supposed to look like.

"Hi. Uh, bonjour. Je suis Prince. Je suis un ami avec Enzo."

The man that answered the door was a few shades darker than me with a hightop fade. The whites of his eyes were bright and he stared back with a vague cheeriness.

"You are who? You speak English?"

I wiped my hand off on my jacket and held it out for him to shake, then spoke as I showed him the paper. "Yes. I'm Prince. My friend in the US said she emailed Enzo and said that it was okay for me to stay here. Is this the right address?"

He stared at the paper for a moment, nodded, and opened the door farther.

"Come on. My name is Kleo. I am from Africa. You are Africa American? You would like a beer?"

I stepped through the doorway into a small living room with couches that had cloth draped over them. Four bookshelves walled in the dining room area. French African teenagers walked by on the street outside. A cat jumped onto the couch near me and purred. I sipped my beer and sank into the couch with a sigh. The excitement of arriving in a new country had quickly faded as soon as I stepped out of the airport and started sweating. I struggled to decipher the directions for the RER train to Enzo's house.

I hadn't expected to feel so deflated, so I took a nap after I finished my beer. I awoke on the couch with other people buzzing around the living room and dining room, speaking a language I didn't know. Numerous people introduced themselves to me—a woman with warm skin and long, brown hair, a tall white man with a gravel-like voice and beard, and a shorter Brazilian girl with small hands and a big smile. It was nearing dinner when I sat at the table and had already quantified in my mind how many days (nineteen exactly) I'd have to stomach the discomfort of being around these new strange people.

During the dinner, a thin boy in a striped, long-sleeved shirt sat at the table. He kissed his friend, another roommate, on the cheek and held her hand, then laughed as she made a joke. She gestured in my direction and he leaned forward. His face was an open canvas under a head of fluffy black hair.

"You are Melissa's friend, Prince? Enchanté. C'est Enzo. Ça va?"

I tried to stop the stirring in my head, both from trying to decipher French and the color of his eyes.

I smiled back and replied, "Yes. Thank you so much for letting me stay here. It's really nice."

I quickly realized that the twenty phrases of French that I'd scribbled into my notebook weren't good enough to navigate staying in a household of people that had immigrated to France over the last few years. My face got warm every time I met someone and forgot to kiss them on both cheeks. Even going to the grocery store was a hassle when I had to decide what item to buy that was past my visual recognition of the product. I had a list of activities as options for things that I could do on a given day.

My second day in Paris, I took the train to the center of the city, bought a bottle of wine, drank heavily under the Eiffel Tower, and walked to its second level. Children ran around in their jackets and scarves. It was a warm April day, so the entire city was in view on all sides. I tried to blink the tears away from my eyes as a holy feeling washed over me, filling my entire body. I wasn't sure how to process this ancestral trek, a Black person, in a land that had aided in the Atlantic Slave Trade and had displayed my people as effective animals to be prodded in a zoo. But some part of me was dedicated to seeing this journey through in order to make sense of it as best as I could.

■ ■ ■

On my first night in Paris, Enzo's friends invited me to a party on a nearby university campus. I stumbled through helping them sell wine and beer. A short German student fixated on me and sat near the table of everyone selling booze in the courtyard.

"I want to practice my English. Tell me about the political condition in America," he requested.

We talked late into the party and he pressed me further and further on my beliefs. I talked about high school and my teacher making our class read the *Communist Manifesto*. I talked about my parents rejecting me after I came out to them. Anthony Sowell had lived on my aunt's street and murdered numerous Black women, a demographic made invisible by the state. All of this taught me that I wanted more than what America could give me. I wanted a society that didn't necessitate surpluses of goods in exchange for most of the planet being relegated to poverty. I believed that revolution, socialism, then communism could lead to that.

"So you are a Marxist?" he sneered.

I nodded faintly and thought of the question as I was leaving, realizing that I had worn the label like a second skin for a number of years, but something in his assumption bothered me. I thought of it on the car ride back to Enzo's house. On the way, he brushed another car on the highway and attempted to drive off. The other car sped up after us, turned into our path, and cut the brakes. I watched from the back seat as the driver of the other car, a woman with frazzled blonde hair, yelled at Enzo. The near wreck felt like a strange omen during this grand trip, a dark marker that told me to step further into the unknown.

I traveled to Chambery and visited my college friend, Olga, who was teaching English there. We trekked to the former home of philosopher Jean-Jacques Rousseau and watched the sunset in the neighboring garden filled with yellow flowers. We went clubbing and met a guy named Clemente, who invited us to his apartment. While we smoked weed, he debated with me about what amount of hope I had for the future of America. Although I argued, I didn't tell him the entire truth, which was that hope seemed like a pretty flimsy prerequisite for political change. In some ways, there had to be a certain kind of desperation involved as well.

The next day, I peeled myself away and took a bus while hungover to Lyon. I arrived in the afternoon to a glittering and stacked town. I walked through inclined streets and between restaurants, lit orange and loud with the clattering forks of patrons.

My hostel for the first two nights was on a hill with a stony outside balcony that overlooked canals, churches, and drawbridges. On the last night there, I met up with a friend, went to a bar, and planned to kill time before my bus back to Paris. My friend, who was studying abroad, had to get back to her host family's home before curfew. I started to close my tab and leave the wooden bar.

"Wait. Are you American?" said a voice from the other end of the bar.

I looked over and saw a girl. She introduced herself as Bethany.

"You're here alone?" she said as she leaned her chin onto her hand and smiled mischievously. "You should meet up with me and some other Americans."

Bethany took me to bars with her other friends, all white Americans studying abroad. They were nice and smiling and drinking. I was glad to be in their presence, to speak English with other people from the same country as me. Bethany was from New York and mentioned her sister who acted in *Twin Peaks* more than a few times. The conversation at the table froze when she got to the topic of going back to the States soon.

"You've got to be careful about the Muslims here," she said in my direction. "There's really a lot of violence in that community."

I pursed my lips and adjusted my legs beneath the table. Everyone averted their gazes or sipped their drinks. I didn't.

"That's not cool to say."

She elaborated. One night she had been walking home and came upon a Muslim couple arguing. The woman started screaming at her, then the man rushed forward and shoved her. She went plummeting down a flight of stairs, terrified as they loomed above her.

"That's fucked up that that happened to you, but it doesn't give you a right to generalize about Muslims anywhere. Do you know what Muslims have gone through in the United States since 9/11?"

She shrugged and sipped her drink. She was returning to New York soon, taking a break from school, and living with her parents. By the end of the night, Bethany offered to let me crash on her couch. The clarity of her comments and the way her friends averted their gazes almost made me laugh. White people yield so much power because of structural racism, yet seldom acknowledge or challenge each other. James Baldwin had written about it in *Notes of a Native Son*: "Though the students of any nation, in Paris, are allowed irresponsibility, few seem to need it as desperately as Americans seem to need it; and none, naturally, move in the same aura of power, which sets up in the general breast a perceptible anxiety, and wonder, and a perceptible resentment."

I took a bus back to Paris a few days later, wedged in my seat and finished *Assata: An Autobiography*. The countryside shot by. I tried to make sense of the distance from Ohio, my home, my friends, and here. I opened my journal and wrote a poem that partially read, "maybe we will forget/the scars of a branded land/a branded rest/a Black child sold for slaughter?/ but maybe we don't want to."

...

I soon met other Americans that were traveling and crashing at Enzo's house during my time in Europe. Ben wore cargo pants and camouflage shirts. He kept his hair in a ponytail and was more of a listener than a talker. Ben came to Europe to travel and understand the political situation among different groups of comrades. I felt a kinship with him; we were both Americans who left our country for the first time to learn something new in another place.

"Are you going to the Nuit Debout demonstrations?" he asked me.

We sat at a table outside of Enzo's house. I smoked a cigarette that I had borrowed from someone inside and tried to soothe myself in the day's heat. I'd read a bit online about the movement that had just started a month before I'd arrived in the country. I hadn't, however, decided how to engage as a temporary visitor.

Nuit Debout was considered by many to be a part of a wave of global movements, partially in reaction to how the Great Recession was affecting economic, political, and labor policies in countries all around the world. The Occupy movement had been in my peripheral vision, something I assumed many white people participated in as their first entryway into the radical tradition. Over time I realized that it awakened many

Americans to the looming evils of capitalism. Hollande's government proposed a series of changes to labor in the country under the El Khomri Law, like reducing overtime payments, making it easier for companies to lay off workers, and lowering severance payments.

"There were hundreds of thousands of people marching in the streets just a week ago," Ben asserted. "It's pretty serious. You should come out with me."

I knew that I couldn't travel all this way and decline his offer because I wasn't sure of what to expect. Everyone else in the house seemed prepared in one way or another—jackets with inside pockets stuffed with extra handkerchiefs or Maalox (which helped with the tear gas when mixed with water), sometimes actual gas masks, or even bags with beer to enjoy whatever destruction would come along the way. I learned that a trial was currently happening in France to decide the fate of two officers that chased two teens who hid in a transformer at an electrical substation and were electrocuted. Only a year later, mass unrest occurred after Adama Traoré, an unarmed twenty-four-year-old, was killed while fleeing police in a suburb of Paris.

The next Saturday, the movement's weekly day of protest, Ben and I took the RER to Place de la République. Once there, I stuffed my handkerchief into my pocket and scanned the area. The crowd was mostly teenagers and people in their early twenties.

"It's more common for police here to just beat the shit out of you and leave. In the US, a lot of people say the cops are real hungry for arrests," Ben noted as the day's march started.

The crowd of roughly three thousand people took to the streets. Ben and I walked in a section of the crowd filled with Parisian teenagers that looked far more stylish than anyone I'd seen at a protest in the US, with hair tied back in colorful scrunchies, crisp white shoes, and Adidas track pants.

"Just keep your eyes open. If you're ever too uncomfortable or want to find a way out, let me know. I've been to a few of these things and want to make sure you don't feel like you're freaking out," he said as he looked at me.

Ahead of us, the crowd jeered as a puff of gray smoke wafted out of a building a few blocks down. Ben tied his Maalox-soaked handkerchief around his face and so did I. Up ahead, more screams and chaos surfaced. At an intersection, the black bloc used broken street rails and detached mailboxes to form a soft line against the police. A silver orb fell down about ten feet away from us and pepper shot into the air.

The crowd all around us lurched as Ben grabbed onto my arm and pulled me away. We wandered the madness in the same delirium as everyone else that had shown up that day—wandering down one alleyway to make a turn and be met with a dead end, backing away as scuffles broke out ahead, or climbing telephone poles to get a better view.

People in black tagged buildings with spray paint, used broken handrails to smash ATM screens, and lobbed rocks at storefront windows. Behind us, French police swung their batons at falling protesters or beat them against their shields. A woman in a white scarf went down from an officer's swing and then was sucked through the police line by her legs as she screamed.

I ran faster to catch up with Ben. A gaggle of us reached a side street. I stopped, grateful to have a moment to breathe and cursing myself for forgetting my inhaler. I coughed and wiped the sweat away from my face.

I opened my mouth to tell him that I'd never seen anyone be yanked behind a line of police like that when Ben grabbed my hand. He jerked hard and whipped me backward. I gasped from the shock as my feet caught up and a loud metal crunch rose up behind me.

Policemen had pulled up a barricade to block the path that Ben pulled me away from. Someone else grabbed a metal pole and slammed it into a car's windshield, sending the alarm's blare down the alleyway. The chaos of the images from the Freddie Gray protests of the last year flooded my mind and suddenly connected with the images right in front of me.

All of the speeches and discussions I'd listened to while scrubbing toilets and fixing beds spoke and told my thumping heart that this was not the only wreckage that I would see. Soon it was the throngs of people spilling out of side streets into the main streets, with nowhere to use the bathroom or sit down or close your eyes.

As we continued to walk, Ben glanced ahead and behind us, tapping my arm sometimes when something in the vicinity seemed off. I swallowed a lump in my throat and thought of the first question to ask when the people around us quieted down.

"How'd you learn about all this?"

Ben talked about how inspiring the Occupy movement, which rose to international prominence in 2011, was for the ways that it brought people from different ends of the lower economic spectrum together, despite its problems with sexual assault and counterinsurgent infiltration. Ben explained, "It was the first time in my life where it wasn't just some idea in my head. I could see the way things could change right in front of me."

After a few hours, our section of the crowd crossed a bridge after being kettled in a side street for over an hour. The foot traffic was heavy up ahead and even heavier behind us. A separate and recently attacked contingent joined our mass. A teenage boy with curly black hair grabbed onto my shoulder and I held him up by his armpit. He couldn't open his eyes. His face was bright red. He spoke quickly, weakly.

"Avez-vous Maalox? Avez-vous l'eau, s'il vous plait?"

I struggled to respond for the next block or so as he tried to peel his eyes open with his hands. Ben was close by, but not within sight. I skimmed the crowd for medics and realized that most of them had scattered to help people with worse injuries. As this stranger and I struggled along while holding on to each other, I realized part of the importance of this kind of protest: the strangeness of coming together as strangers to experience a very real, but sometimes hidden violence. In some ways, this seemed to be the very effect of feeling like I'd fallen into a pot hole that the state and the police wanted to imbue. Eventually the teenager's friend came to carry him off.

The demonstration ended where it started, at Place de la République. Protesters stomped over the candles and photos left for the people killed in the November 2015 terrorist attack as police rained down canisters of tear gas. I ran and nearly slipped on a canister before someone pulled me up. My face burned like someone had just dumped hot sauce on it. I almost didn't want to open my mouth for fear that the sweat pouring down my face would get into my mouth and burn there too.

A stranger grabbed me and poured the relieving liquid onto my eyes. I hadn't even fully regained my vision and started to say "Merci" before I realized that the person who had helped me was already gone to help the next chemically ravaged person. For the first real time that day, I settled into the terror all around me as some part of me thought of Baldwin when he said, "It is innocence which constitutes the crime."

■ ■ ■

A few days later, Enzo and his friends attended another day of protests while I roamed another part of the city on my own. When I returned to Enzo's home, everyone was in a mood. They spoke seriously around the dining room table about a friend's arrest during that day's protests. I tried to sit, not forcing myself to comprehend the minimal vocabulary that I knew, and instead matched their somber air. I walked to the store before the evening turned to soft rain and bought bottles of wine. Enzo and I were the last ones at the table. Talking, drinking, and gazing at each other as the rain sang outside.

"I want to spend as much time with you as I can before you leave," he said.

He put on the film *Wild at Heart*. It depicted the riotous journey of Nicolas Cage through lust and debauchery. I remember red tones, long driving scenes, and a sultry blonde woman. I remember Enzo's shoulder touched mine as we sat beneath a blanket, then him inviting me to his bed. His body was slimmer then I'd imagined as we rolled around in the dimness of his room.

At the time, I almost refused to believe that the romance could be more than what it was. The next day, the city was bright as we traveled into it. We roamed thrift stores. He took me through the steps of trying to steal the clothes that I wanted. Our efforts failed miserably, but he smiled as I laughed and laughed and laughed. Over Lebanese food, I rambled about my favorite movies within earshot of the people at the countless tables all around us. I tied a scarf that I had gotten that day around his head and he blushed as I laughed again.

I loved how he shivered when I touched certain parts of his body—behind the ears, the right buttock, the skin beneath his belly button. Late at night, he opened his bedroom windows as we lay in sweat. The outside world rolled over us with the sounds of ambulance sirens, car horns, and friends shouting late at night. I savored it all. On the drive to the airport, we listened to Jackson 5 and I stared in awe as he rolled cigarettes while driving. We rushed into a photo booth at the airport and kissed as the camera snapped. When it was time to say goodbye, we hugged and I forced myself to walk away, to not look back. I left the notebook where I wrote about all the little moments with him on my last flight back to Cleveland, an accident and a lost archival.

"I really liked him," I said to my friend Jericho while sucking down stiff drinks at a bar while visiting my college town.

Everyone back home wanted to know the details of my glorious trip abroad. I rattled off the list of things that I'd done. Most people nodded in response and then their eyes glazed over. My time in Yellowstone, all the excitement upon my re-turn, and then the ephemeral questions afterward taught me that most people didn't know how to conceptualize talking about travel and the deep wounds that it can leave you. Jericho was the first person to press me on my connection with Enzo. I tried to breathe slowly as I answered.

"I really, really liked him. It was like I . . . didn't need to be anything more than what I was. It was fun."

Jericho slapped a hand on my shoulder.

"It's okay if you loved him. You can say it," he replied.

By August, the business of France seemed far away. I had been back in the United States for a number of months. I returned to Montana to work another season as a housekeeper at the same resort from the summer before and quickly found myself unsatisfied with most of my coworkers. It could have been lessons from Yellowstone or the things that I had seen. Something in me had changed. The ugliness culminated when I went to a party with my white friend, Ashley, and her boyfriend, who was also my boss during my third month of work. My boss told racist jokes, which he deemed ironic when we hung out. On the night of the party, I was particularly annoyed when a Mex-ican dude said the n-word casually. Drunk on vodka, I snapped.

"If anyone in this room ever says that word, there's going to be a fucking problem," I spat.

Everyone stared back like I'd grown another head.

"Don't worry about Prince y'all," Marco, a black coworker, said. "He just angry at the whole world, so he can't have fun."

"Marco, I'm sorry that your family made you so white that you're actually a house slave," I said with the sharpest part of my mind perking up. As I kept on talking, I made eye contact with the subject of my anger. The sneering Mexican dude was next. "Go back to Mexico and be racist there. Fuck you."

I turned to Ashley and said, "You are such a coward and I hope you never talk to another Black person in your life."

I took another long swig of my vodka and stormed out of the room, hoping that the silence I left behind ruined the rest of their night. I quit my job a few days later after sobbing on the phone to Kelli in a bathroom and moved into a basement room of a friend's house in my college town. I took a job as a lead organizer for a political group encouraging people to vote responsibly for the environment.

"Did you hate the last organizing job that you had?" Nadia challenged me over the phone.

I tried to ignore that life was repeating itself. I decided my need for the money necessitated my ignorance and innocence. Pretty soon the money wasn't worth the endless days and the lunch breaks where I'd walk the three blocks to my house to get stoned. Every strategy my job wanted to deploy seemed straight out of a *What Can White Men Say about Organizing the Youth* manual. I quit on a sunny fall day and fantasized about hitchhiking to Florida. My friends and I started to spray-paint and steal American flags. We burned the flags in our backyards while drinking malt liquor. Donald Trump's antics flooded the news streams. We all laughed, but a different kind of gravity was taking hold of my entire body.

I concocted a plan when I learned that Bill Clinton was coming to Athens, Ohio, to give a speech on behalf of Hillary Clinton's presidential campaign. I gathered my friends and printed off quarter sheets with facts about the 1994 Violent Crime and Prevention Bill, which expanded the death penalty, initiated the "three strikes, you're out" rule for felony offenders, and incentivized the expansion of correctional facilities nationwide. Hillary Clinton had been a notable advocate for the bill, when she called Black youth "superpredators" in 1996.

My comrades and I canvassed the line of people waiting to go in and then entered the event. College Green was filled with thousands of people wearing Hillary hats and holding their children. America's tyranny was boiling over once more. America loved to disguise death as anything but death.

Bill Clinton walked onstage and started his speech. The audience clapped. I waited for my moment and screamed wide, "I will not vote for candidates that have sent millions of my people to prison. I will not vote for a fake democracy that is dependent upon my silence. I will not vote for candidates that use white feminism to destroy and disrespect Black lives."

Parts of the crowd attempted to chant over me, telling me to let Clinton speak. A white volunteer for the Clinton campaign approached me, tried to gesture for me to leave. I continued to shout, even as a cop approached. I kept shouting as I walked out with all the beady eyes of white people staring at me with confusion, disgust, or calm. I stared back at as many of them as I could and tried to convey with my eyes, Don't you fucking care what this country has done? Don't you have a soul?

But I knew the answer.

I rushed out of the speech, went to a nearby building, and changed into a new set of clothes. I kept my head low and got back into the event. Immediately another white campaign volunteer grabbed my arm. I tried to listen for the shouts of my friends that said they would disrupt too. I couldn't hear them.

I sped out of the event, pushing past as many people as I could before a cop might find me. My friends found me outside, resting by a tree.

"How did it go for y'all?" I asked.

They all kind of shrugged. One of them replied, "Well, we didn't really disrupt. We kind of yelled, but no one asked us to leave."

After the speech, I noticed the people around me moving in a different way. The same white friends that had rejected the idea of the disruption were either silent or inquired faintly about what happened. While out for drinks at a bar, a white friend stopped me, looked me in the eyes, and said, "You know. You're really important and all of this really scares me. I'm worried for your safety."

Nails and barbed wire grated against the pit of my stomach. Despite all of the existential anxiety that came with the leaps of faith involved in leaving Seattle, going to Paris, and nearly falling in love, I'd learned that the first step to having a chance at changing the world was to take my body back and thrust myself toward things that made me feel alive. I could do that again and again, so that doing things like disrupting the speeches of former presidents wouldn't be so bizarre. By now I'd learned the importance of being incompatible with a world that aimed to destroy you.

Standing Rock, North Dakota, United States, 2016

The dream ended like a hammer slamming down on my throat. The force of it bulged my eyes open, contracted my throat, and jolted me awake as I scrambled for the backseat door handle. I stumbled outside, thankful that we were in a parking lot and not on some highway en route to North Dakota. I stared out at the expansive dull green of the roadside off of the McDonald's parking lot. It was early October of 2016. My tongue swelled in my mouth. A heat moved through me, lighting up my insides.

In the dream, I was at a vigil at the graffiti wall in Athens, Ohio. People stood all around, crying into their sleeves and laying candles down. I knelt to put my own candle down. The realization moved through me like a pack of leeches. I looked up. It was my older brother's face painted on the mural. He had been shot dead in some alleyway, first running, then shouting, feeling the sharp heat as the bullets tore through him. Those white mouths laughing in their blue uniforms.

My breath, cold and hoarse, came to my body through the dream as I woke up in the back seat; it was the kind of breath before all of the memories and impossibility and delirium kicks in. The sobs took over my body in the back seat. It drizzled in the McDonald's parking lot as I put my phone to my ear.

"Hello?" Nadia answered groggily.

I talked too fast and not quickly enough at all. I crouched beneath the awning of the McDonald's, which was opening up for the day. I stared ahead past the asphalt parking lot and toward the open sheets of dim green land. My head throbbed and my throat swelled. Nadia told me to slow down, to breathe. I couldn't.

"I don't know what I'm doing here. I don't know why the fuck any of us are doing this. Why the fuck am I doing this?"

Ty're King, a thirteen-year-old Black boy who weighed one hundred pounds, was out with his friends in their neighborhood in Columbus, Ohio. Police suspected him and his friends of a ten-dollar robbery and chased them down. They cornered King and one of his friends in an alleyway and claimed he pulled out a gun from his waistband. He was pronounced dead at a nearby hospital at 8:22 p.m. on September 16, 2016. An independent autopsy contracted by his family showed that King was running away when he was shot by Officer Bryan Mason. I organized a public memorial for him in Athens, Ohio, which was an hour away from Columbus, and stayed for hours as white people walked by, glanced for a moment, and went on about their day.

A white guy came up to me as I stared at the candles set down on the courthouse steps. He wanted to apologize for the loss of Ty're, froze in place, and then said, "Why remove the blame for Ty're? We wouldn't do that for Osama Bin Laden."

My body short-circuited. I screamed. My white friends watched, shaken by my anger. I wanted to destroy his whiteness, his ignorance with my voice. With my hands. To him, we were just more Black bodies to enrich the land, more death to feed the white lips of an always hungry America. I was tired of us dying, and worse, of watching us die. I was tired of feeling trapped by the horror of it.

"I don't know how we survive this," I said to Nadia.

"Some of us don't."

I thought of Aunt Vick's words—"Some have to die so that others can live."

But who chooses who lives, I thought, and why had I made it so far?

After talking to Nadia on the phone in McDonald's parking lot and continuing my journey to Standing Rock, I arrived at a camp just outside of Oceti Sakowin after nightfall with a sense of dread. This first camp was smaller and had about eight people. They immediately filled me in about their cynicism about the whole movement, which had been erected by LaDonna Brave Bull Allard to defeat the Black Snake or the Dakota Access Pipeline.

"A lot of the people in that main camp are just a bunch of fucking pussies, lying on us, informing on us," the scruffy Indigenous man named Citrus said at the night fire. "People come here and think this movement is about truth and liberation. For a lot of them, it's about wanting to tell a pretty little story."

My friend Samantha and I had quit our organizing job on the same day a week before. We ran giddily into the office, dropped off our supplies, and mused about what to do next. I paid keen attention on social media to the Standing Rock movement and knew that something was about to happen.

America was heading toward a massive cliff with shot-up churches; undrinkable water in Flint, Michigan; the bloodied, tangled dance floor of Pulse nightclub; and the destruction of fentanyl, which ended the life of the singer, Prince, and so many others.

I didn't know if the political solution to our pressing times was to ride out whatever project you were already invested in, contribute to whichever movements wanted you, or a complicated mix of both. I'd met enough well-read socialists sitting around in book clubs to know that I wanted to act and not just read. But acting, nonetheless, was far more complicated than most people made it out to be.

I awoke the next morning on the roadside of Highway 1806, which was parallel to Oceti Sakowin and Sacred Stone Camp just down the road. The sky was a soft orange and yellow. I put on my boots after stepping into the dewy grass with my socks. Our camp was a smattering of tents: one for the kitchen, another for the supply tent, and another for resources. All of which were susceptible to the rain. We drank burnt coffee and ate cereal over the morning fire.

"Let's get the fuck out of this depressing camp," I mumbled to Samantha. We packed our bags then walked the half a mile to Oceti Sakowin with a woman who had been live-streaming the movement from the beginning. She was heavyset with dyed blonde hair and a warmth that contrasted the previous night.

"I'm a live-streamer, not a journalist," she said. "But when the feds get you, they've gotta give you some kind of label, some kind of position to justify surveying you. There's only so much of your phone not working or hearing clicks on the other line that can happen before you know something fishy is going down."

I was mesmerized by her conviction as a mother working to shield her children from the impact of her numerous arrests. In my heart, I felt like a trembling child that just wanted the world to be a better place. Meeting this woman helped me believe that that may be possible, even if it was in some minute way.

"The things that those pigs said to me while I was being detained? Fat bitch this and fat bitch that. We're gonna take your phone and find out what those Indians are doing."

Samantha and I set up our tents in Oceti Sakowin just off the camp's main path, which was lined with flags fluttering in the morning light. Children ran around. The scale of the land was massive with cars, camps, tents, and horses that spread out for at least another mile. Samantha and I were keen to see the other camps in the area, specifically Sacred Stone Camp, which was where the Standing Rock movement was started.

While on the walk there, we neared a group of other people our age. A tall woman with dark-brown hair eyed me, then introduced herself as Zofi. She was from St. Louis. This was her third and last day here before she returned to classes. We trekked our way up to Sacred Stone through more tents, camps, RVs, and fires. The hilltop was mostly empty, aside from a makeshift cabin that was also a security entrance.

While walking back into Oceti Sakowin, Zofi and I shared our experiences with each other, she as a trans woman of color and I as a queer Black man. An Indigenous security man in a black cap snickered as we walked by, then chided, "Didn't know people were coming here to be gay."

I rolled my eyes and bit my tongue as my face flushed with heat. I knew that if I lashed out now, the situation could become a powder keg. The camp got dark. Samantha returned to our tent and I decided to accompany Zofi to the Queer Camp. Their shaved heads, thick boots, and eccentric clothing made me feel at home. I crossed my arms and pressed in close with a circle of them.

"Is this how it really is here? Was what that man said at the gate normal?" I asked.

The person that answered had short black hair and smoked a drag of her cigarette, then shrugged.

"You know how it is. We all do. I'm Indigenous. I'm here to throw down, but there are gaps in it. Some people tell women not to walk around alone after dark. We fucking know what that means. Some shit is being covered up. We can exist to fulfill a role, but we can't fully be ourselves."

I couldn't shake the shiver that her reasoning sent down my spine. Suddenly I was in that parking lot at fifteen years old and staring down my mother as I told her that our family's homophobia growing up had forced me to protect myself and hide my identity. I wished that I could have gone back and let my mouth fall open in almost intrigued disbelief as she said, "But those things we said weren't about you. We never meant to hurt you."

They'd demanded to know why I chose my individuality over my prescribed role in the family. This was the first moment that I realized that I could exist for them, but only in a way that was digestible to them. The price of the ticket to enter my family was at the expense of shaving off the parts of myself that had seemingly taught me the most about life and fallibility of people. There was no room to hold my pain in a family that wanted to move forward and hold together an illusion.

The person in the camp saw the disappointment on my face and then offered me a cigarette. I knew I couldn't start saying everything that was in my head because if I started talking, I simply wouldn't stop. It didn't make sense to me that a movement built on anti-colonialism would still hand down soft rules to tell people how to use/present their bodies. The security man's words effectively translated to, "Fuck you, you fucking faggot. We don't need you here."

But I had come here to learn. I was Black and not Indigenous. I was poor but had graduated from college with a mound of debt. It wasn't my job to parachute in, label all the problems within my first day, and deem an entire movement toxic.

"This is what we do, you know?" the girl said. "We find our family. We show up. We put in the work where we can. When they reject us or don't want to see us, we have each other."

Her words calmed me, but as I trudged back to my tent and lay down next to Samantha, I was also aware that my new friends were leaving the next day. I'd be forced to navigate the rest of my time there without a queer confidant.

For the rest of my week, I threw myself into doing whatever tasks I could find. Samantha and I volunteered at the school after its teacher found us eying work teams on the camp's bulletin board. The school was inside of two massive teepees. The first one held books, art supplies, and whatever snacks were nonperishable. The second teepee had tables and chairs for the children to sit at.

The thin, brown-haired teacher gazed at Samantha and asked, "So can you teach science, de-colonial history, what?"

"We're not really . . . licensed."

"Teaching licenses," the woman replied back to Samantha as she grabbed a clipboard from a nearby table, "are a colonial construct."

We caught the drift. Over the next week and a half, Samantha and I did our best to wrangle the children and read whatever books they requested. We started the day with math and science lessons before going into the more free-form activities of the evening. Forest was a spunky six-year-old. He often ran around with his shirt off, finding the hatchet that his father gifted him, puffing his chest and shouting, "Kill the black snake! Ahoooo!" Samantha and I darted between lawn chairs and tents to chase him down as people watched in bewilderment. Whenever we were caught, we sighed with relief after not tumbling down near a child with a hatchet. There was the five-year-old girl that seemed to be a transplant from some yuppie family. She had a high ponytail and pouted whenever anyone said anything to her. That was until I offered to jump rope with her. For my next few days at the camp, she latched onto me any chance that she got.

It was important to live in the moment while in Standing Rock. Some who arrived to Oceti Sakowin shallowly mused that we were experiencing an Indigenous utopia and believed there could be a genuine return to a pre-capitalist life.

I didn't want to romanticize an entire movement, but I was in awe. No money was spent while we were there. Numerous teams of a dozen people volunteered throughout the day to cook meals in the different camps. Whenever you did anything at all around the camp, even collecting trash, you were told, "Do what you do with love. Whatever is in your heart transfers into what you do."

On one of our first days in camp, a burning voice came over the loudspeaker. It yelled, "All warriors to the front lines!"

Plates of food were shoveled down and left. People climbed into pickup trucks. Samantha and I gazed at each other. We set our plates down without speaking. After a long bus ride, we reached the pipeline, where an Indigenous tree-planting ceremony and prayer occurred. Another flank of water protectors were in the distance, jumping over ditches and distracting the workers, who weren't allowed to build with intruders present. Intruders, I thought; America and capitalism has turned Indigenous peoples into intruders.

Pretty soon, we were all running, avoiding the TigerSwan security as they swarmed. They looked short and white and heavy as they jogged toward us wearing sunglasses, black polo shirts, and tan shorts. Energy Transfer Partners, the company behind the Dakota Access Pipeline, had hired TigerSwan, a private security company to protect its assets.

I took a ride back to Ohio with a woman named Whitney driving home to Michigan. She talked a lot on the twenty-hour drive back to the Midwest about her grief and the anger of her activism in her twenties, which she described as, "I was just angry at everything. I look at how people interact with each other today and it doesn't make any sense. No one is listening to each other."

On a trip to South America, she sweated through a peyote trip for numerous days as her late brother visited her and she fought to grapple with her grief. For a moment, a ball of warmth spread through my chest for her because she, too, had been wounded by death. The warmth, however, could not shake my wariness about what she was expressing about anger and progress. America had already taught me that rage was so often dictated by the reality that one is born into. A white woman's rage at America was different from my own. After all, who filled the jail cells the most when they were not polite, patient, or willing to police the emotions of others? Could she ever relate to how being Black meant that I had to face and know and embody death?

As she spoke, I sank farther into my seat and sometimes looked out at the scenery turning from flat roadsides to sky-scrapers to woodsy, rural roads. Eventually, we reached the topic of why I had left my state to join a movement so far away. In a way, I couldn't explain it all, but I could connect my answer to loss, to my loss that was both amorphous and jagged.

"I don't know," I said, fearful that I might fall asleep and also because some other, strange dream was edging toward me, "part of me looks at all of these places that I'm going to and the places I've been. I enjoy it. I love it. I feel grateful and I'm glad to push myself, but I get this weird feeling."

"What feeling?"

It was raining and she white-knuckled the steering wheel. I couldn't recall what state we were in, but it was late. The high-ways had cleared significantly. Now there were only trucks and a sky unable to birth any stars. The world beyond us was frozen. In a way, we were stateless, and this statelessness took me back to months before. Months before when my late-night flight arrived in Big Sky, Montana. After grabbing my bags from the small carousel, I stepped outside to see no cars. I sighed, realizing suddenly that I had not one, but two white friends who had failed to pick me up from the airport.

With only fifty dollars and a dead phone, I realized I didn't have a way to take a taxi, to call anyone, or to even afford a hotel for the night. Under the darkened sky, I walked out to the wide grass field in front of the airport, set my sleeping bag down, and fell asleep. I awoke, soaked in dew, and marveled at the orange and fuchsia morning sky.

Now back in the car with Whitney as we barreled down the highway, I told the truth. "I wish I could take people with me. I wish I could reach back and yank every single person I've cared about to see the waterfall or even, the sky at night in the camp. I hadn't seen that many stars in a while. Sometimes it feels like I'm carrying this whole crowd of people, whose world I want to change, whose world I hope would change if they came with me. I wish there was a name for that feeling."

Then his face came into my mind, first a blur. Then as clear as it has been when he'd come to me in a dream where I was being chased through a hospital. He shoved me toward a safe exit as hands, arms, and limbs swallowed him.

"It makes me think of my father, what it would have been like to know him. If he'd be proud of me." Or I thought, if he and I could ever be more than mysteries to each other.

"He would proud of you," she tried to smile at me. "I'm sure of it."

I didn't know what to say, so the car went silent for a while. It always irked me when people proposed that parents, whether dead or alive, only loved their children unconditionally. I'd seen the ugly side of an unconditional love turned somewhat conditional. It was the blade digging deeper and deeper into my back, fusing into how I stood and faced the world. If my father were alive, it would be naive to assume he would accept a gay son. White people or non-queer people can afford living lives based on such illusions.

I was nearly asleep when she turned down the radio and cleared her throat.

"I know this might be weird for me to say. I feel like you have a very strong spirit and the way that you've talked about your father, there seems to be something there. You mentioned that dream in the hallway that you always had as a child, right?"

I nodded. Her expression was consumed in thought. My stomach dropped. Then she replied, "Have you ever considered talking to someone who could help you communicate with your father?"

■ ■ ■

I returned to Standing Rock two weeks later with more people and more supplies. Fall was in full effect and the political repression happening in Standing Rock was all over the news. After my first trip to Standing Rock, many of my friends were curious about what I had experienced during my time there.

"Oh, you know, lots of cooking and cleaning and I helped take care of the kids at the main camp a lot," I usually replied.

It was common for the person to say "how cool" it was that I had the free time to go. I understood the sentiment, but also wondered what it would take for people in the United States, especially young, privileged, and able-bodied people to drop their social responsibilities to join a cause because of pure, political grit. I couldn't quite answer how exactly I'd come to be in this mode of living, but I was sure that I couldn't really go back. Everything that I'd witnessed thus far and the dream in the car had uprooted me, put me in my place.

In Athens, I became good friends with Emma and Angela. We drank in bar bathrooms, gave each other drunken stick n' poke tattoos, and became a little family. With the oncoming presidential election and the constant news cycle of destruction and death, we were intent on raising our own hell.

From the moment that I met Emma during my sophomore year of college, she mystified me. Clear skinned and long haired, she wrote poetry about rural Ohio and had a gathered, but stoic energy about her. When I returned to Ohio after Montana, we gravitated toward each other, two radicals trying to orient ourselves in a crumbling world. I felt like one of her confidants. She felt like a partner in crime. We laughed as we coached our friends to burn flags. I scribbled paint and marker onto a jacket that I found in a clothing pile at Oceti Sakowin camp and wore the new piece of clothing all the time. A few times a week, a white person came up to me in public and demanded an answer to why I'd written "Fuck White America" on the back of it. I usually stared back at them in mock confusion and went about my day.

The three of us returned to Standing Rock for my second trip. This time, the mood was drastically different. We stayed with comrades who had been camping for weeks and talked extensively to us over the night fire pit about how heavily peace policing was affecting the movement.

"You show up to the front lines ready to throw down and suddenly there's an Indigenous dude or a white dude grabbing the rock out of your hand, ripping the handkerchief off of your face."

There were other stories too. A girl that I met went to the front lines wearing shorts and an older woman ran up behind her, then wrapped an American flag around her waist. My friends, who were non-binary and had arrived at the camp in a separate car, got stares occasionally when they walked through certain camps. Rumors and suspicions about the motives of the police became more commonplace.

"If you have Verizon, don't even bring your phone here," someone said. "They have cell phone towers that download software onto your device."

In 1996, Bill Clinton signed the Emergency Management Assistance Compact into law, which allows states to share resources and emergency personnel in situations of crisis. Because of this, state troopers arrived in North and South Dakota from different counties, cities, and states. Ohioans spread a petition that demanded that Governor Kasich reverse his decision to send roughly three dozen troops to aid the Dakota Access Pipeline company. If you were a protester or a water protector in a run-of-the-mill meeting, you assumed that TigerSwan had infiltrators there too.

This was the side of the political reality that most people couldn't even begin to grasp. The activists hung from balconies by their ankles by federal agents, and illegal home raids, the traumatizing nature of how state surveillance crawls under your skin, the multitude of companies that profited off of counterinsurgency, and ultimately, the realization that the state can swallow you whole.

Fred Hampton was sleeping in a Black Panther Party apartment on the night of December 4, 1969, when Chicago police riddled him and his friends with bullets. One of Hampton's security personnel was later understood to be a police informant, to have drugged Hampton that night, and to have provided details about the apartment's layout. His son, Fred Hampton Jr., who was in his mother's belly during the raid, once said that he was born with America holding a gun to his head. His sentiment materialized before my eyes.

If you ventured within miles of Oceti Sakowin, you were subject to being searched as you passed through vehicle checkpoints.

"Just visiting the area," my friends and I said when our car was stopped. We were let through.

With the Dakota Access Pipeline set to cross four states from North Dakota to Illinois, many Indigenous peoples stepped forward to oppose the pipeline's route through Indigenous sacred burial grounds and the consequences of building the pipeline near reservation waterways. Many water protectors and Indigenous peoples rightfully noted that the affected land belonged to the local tribes under the terms of the Fort Laramie Treaty of 1851. When water protectors and protesters swarmed onto Sacred Stone Camp, the land of LaDonna Brave Bull Allard, the matriarch of the movement, to protect Indigenous land, divisions arose within the camps.

After many talks, I learned the LaDonna Brave Bull Allard was much more radical than people liked to presume, that she'd wanted Red Warrior Camp, the far more militant component of the movement, to be a part of Sacred Stone Camp and to lead the movement in a more significant way. To people like me, Red Warrior Camp had an air of seriousness around it. I couldn't just walk in, rightfully so, because security culture was necessary among peace policing, infiltrators, and a movement trying to defeat a multi-billion-dollar corporation.

While camping in Sacred Stone, I saw other divisions. During a planning meeting to find ways to gain intel on the progress of the pipeline's construction, a white college dropout from Montana spoke most frequently. Everyone else rolled their eyes.

"It's necessary that whoever agrees to this is fast. We can't get caught because someone is too slow or just a pussy."

I declined his offer when he invited me along.

Days later, a meeting was called in Sacred Stone Camp to debrief on camp plans and needs. Near the end of the meeting, a taller Black man stepped into the circle and spoke on the need for everyone to vote for the presidential election. A shiver swept through me as I noticed countless nods of agreement throughout the circle. By some miracle, my jaw stayed shut when the man suggested we "show the police the peaceful way" by gifting them food on the front lines. Months later while scrolling through Twitter, I saw the same Black man disappear behind a line of police after they yanked him from the front lines. The ease with which his Black body was swallowed up seemed to correlate to his willingness or lack thereof to display the more conflicted parts of his Blackness and political identity. I began to wonder more how we steel ourselves back in a world that so easily tries to disappear us.

This clashing of ideals in camp enlivened me, so I wore my denim jacket with even more pride. I was trying to make a call on Facebook Hill, the only place in the camps with working cell service, when a lanky Indigenous man came up to me.

"Can I talk to you?"

I paused before replying, "Who . . . are you?"

His face became more stern as he asked me to walk a few feet away with him. He leaned close.

"What you're wearing is a problem."

I looked at him and started to sweat. He wore sunglasses and camouflage pants. Hard lines filled his face. He may as well have been a cop for all I cared.

"How is it a problem?"

"What's your name?"

I crossed my arms, stared him down, and tried to think of what Emma would do.

"I'm only going to ask you one more—"

"Prince," I replied. "What's your name?"

"You're going to need to take off the jacket."

He left and I kept the jacket on. Then he came back a few minutes later with another man.

"If you wear that jacket in these camps, you will continue to upset the elders."

"So you're here to tell me what I can and can't wear, yet you're against so many of the laws and rulings of this country. That doesn't make any sense. I'm Black. My people have been colonized too."

The two men crossed their arms.

"If you wear the jacket again, you'll be followed. Do you understand?"

Sweat rolled down my temples as they walked away. I gazed around, embarrassed, as I took the jacket off, almost certain that one of the dozen people nearby had been close enough to hear them and do something. I shared the story with my friends later. They were shocked and told me to continue wearing the jacket. I shook my head. This moment was so different, yet so similar to the homophobic remark by the man at the gate on my first day. Once again, I felt the isolation of being a Black anarchist in a movement. My truth, under capitalism and in a world built on anti-Blackness, was considered more violent than how the camera, media, and police distorted my humanity. Should I even be here, I thought more frequently whenever a stranger eyed me in the camp.

More conversations spread around the camp about the fact that we could be raided at any moment. It was normal to hear helicopters' blades sputtering through the sky as I sat in the darkness of my tent at night. For many, the sounds kept them up, but for me, the helicopters' blades were lulling. These feelings came to a head when worry about a raid reached a climax with my friends. As we sat facing each other, our expressions illuminated by lamp glow, they took turns lamenting on how violent the raid would be, how we had to leave immediately, and that the movement was doomed. I tried to crawl inside of myself and reason with them.

"If you want to leave, that's fine, but we can't freak out about everything that people whisper about in camp. This might be exactly what this pipeline company wants."

Soon we learned that the camp that Samantha and I had arrived at weeks before on our first night was repurposed into the 1851 Treaty Camp. It blocked the next part of the pipeline, which would go on to tear through more sacred Indigenous land. Flashlights were aglow in Oceti Sakowin one night. Emma rushed over to Angela and me.

"They're asking as many people as possible to move to that new camp," Emma said. "They say it's gonna be raided in the middle of the night. Are both of you down?"

I wasn't sure what the purpose of me being there was. It was noble, but didn't feel like my moment. My friends and I helped Emma and Angela set up their tent at the new camp. I stared at them for a long time before we exchanged hugs. Drunken evenings at bars and late-night tattoos in my small bedroom were suddenly so far away.

"See you tomorrow?"

"See you tomorrow," they both replied. As I walked away, the night's darkness swallowed them whole behind me.

I felt like crying until I actually did see them the next morning, but nothing around us was calming down. By eleven a.m., warriors were called to the front lines over the loudspeaker. Angela and I hopped onto the back of a pickup truck and made it to a bridge. Indigenous men prayed and Indigenous women went down to the water to do ceremonies. County Road 134 was one line of defense for the newer camp. Tires were thrown onto a fire barricade that held police off. Snipers posted up on the hilltops and shot at men on horseback with rubber bullets. I coughed from the smoke until an old white man gave me his orange bandana.

"There's shit going down on Highway 1806," someone from another truck yelled. "We need people."

Angela and I jumped into the car. A half a mile up from the newly erected camp, there was a line of military vehicles. We ran into the camp and saw the bedlam. People scrambled to save belongings and other people. Food, clothes, and jewelry were scattered across the grass. The massive wooden frame of a kitchen being constructed was toppled over. Behind us, the screams of the mass of people in the road filled the air. I ran into a teepee and helped a woman shove rugs into her van.

"I can't lose these rugs. They've been in my family for years," she said.

Police closed in just a few feet off of the wire gates of the camp with wooden batons in hand. With all of the bodies moving and pushing and fleeing, it was hard to hear and think over the noise. I adjusted the bandana on my face. Emma had run off, so I worked hard to keep sight of Angela.

"If this is getting too crazy, let me know and we can leave," I said to her.

Earlier that day, Angela watched as a Dakota Access Pipeline worker sped toward Oceti Sakowin in a truck. Water protectors ran him off the road and reeled in shock as the man jumped out of the car, then pointed a handgun at the crowd. It was later discovered that he had an AR-15 rifle in the car. Another white man angry at the resistance, ready to do what was necessary.

I scanned the crowd of entangling bodies trying to flee and swallowed the cement ball in my throat.

"Emma!" I shouted.

A drumbeat of panic lit up my insides, sending fire to my throat. Angela spilled out of the camp and onto the highway. My heart raced. I felt like I wanted to sleep, pass out, or sit on my mother's bed. The white men with their uniforms dragged men out of teepees, and put handcuffs on them. I thought of the images from weeks before, dogs attacking protesters protecting sacred land, and how the protesters related to my people's history, like Black children attacked by police dogs in Birmingham in 1963. America was surely good at being a broken record.

On the main road, police continued to push forward, clad in bulletproof vests, face shields, and riot gear. People kicked away tear-gas canisters that were shot into the crowd. A totaled car was pushed into the road. Others tried to set barricade fires, then were stopped by elders because fires were "too violent."

The front line reached a crescendo. I watched as two people pulled a woman back from the line as she screamed, "Just kill me. Kill me if you're going to take my land again."

In the cry from her gut, I heard another truth—when they take your resources or try to obliterate your culture, they are taking your future and all of the children that your future could produce, relegating the ones to the white-hot violence of the world. Her voice ripped me open, spelled out a willingness to meet an end I suddenly wasn't ready to face yet.

I pulled Angela back as a horse in the crowd kicked its legs into the air. Its muscles pulled tight against its skin as it went wild. The police had shot at it with their rubber bullets. We could die out here, I thought, and it could mean nothing.

People screamed, running in all directions, and their faces stretched in blistering panic. We all moved, tripping and stopping and holding our arms out in case other people fell in front of us. Bodies flocked over the butchered land in a wave. Then I stood, frozen in all of the chaos. Standing against the crowd of bodies was Dai Chi, a boy I met during university, as he struggled to carry a massive suitcase. I was taken back to that the smoke-filled living room on the west side of Athens, the throng of slumped bodies on the couch eating food and staring up at the glow-in-the-dark ceiling.

Walking up to Dai Chi felt like fighting through the Red Sea collapsing in on Moses. When we met in the crowd, we stared at each other and muttered introductions. The purity in his dark eyes rose up in me. I wanted to grab his face at the cheekbones and kiss him, kiss us into a better place. Instead we hugged.

"Stay safe," he said before running off with his suitcase.

The whole day was heavy, a living history book. The night was heavier because none of our friends had seen Emma in hours. By the next morning, our suspicions were confirmed. She had been arrested. Now we just had to find out where she was being jailed and get her out.

I collected funds for her bail as we drove the two hours to the jail and fished through her purse for the medicine that she'd demanded that we bring to her. We got to the jail by nightfall. Angela and I went inside. Our sneakers squeaked against the department's floors. The whole place was barren, creepy. We'd learned that so many people had been arrested that day that the police had to send arrestees to numerous facilities. I couldn't stand the image I had of Emma in my mind—no longer smiling or rebellious, but beaten and purpled in some cold room.

We were taken to the second floor by two police officers. I handed them the medicine for Emma. The cop, a hulking white man, shook the bottles, checked one of them, and then sniffed it.

"So you gave this to me? This is yours?"

We both froze, unsure which of us he was talking to. The other cop put his hand on his waistband.

"This bottle has marijuana and paraphernalia in it. Whose is this?"

I knew that if I said it was Emma's, it might complicate her release. I knew that if Angela claimed it, they would be in trouble. My shoulders tensed. I exhaled.

"It's mine," I said.

The cops turned me around, handcuffed me, and read me my rights. I was too scared to say anything else. Angela's voice shook as they said, "Don't worry. Don't worry."

The cops took me to a brightly lit back room and put my belongings in a plastic bag. My mug shot was taken. They turned my body around and took photos of every one of my tattoos. While typing on the computer as I stood before him, the officer booking me said, "You know, I hate where this country is headed. I wish I didn't have to do this to you."

I scoffed as he led me into the holding cell. I had envisioned being arrested so many times. That it would be at a demonstration as I ran through some side street when a cop tackled me or at a bar because some asshole was groping my friend. I expected to scream, pace the room in a simmering rage, implode, and then crumble into the corner. My mind went to James Baldwin, arrested while penniless for a stolen bed sheet shortly after arriving in Paris and laughed at by the audience in the courtroom when he was released. That laughter followed him to his hotel room after and nearly swallowed him whole.

The holding cell was all white with a toilet and sink in the corner. A single metal sheet was nailed to the wall for a bed. It wasn't really a choice that I made in my body, but more of a mental note. Don't cry. This is bullshit, but you don't get to cry. Every few minutes, I eyed the camera in the ceiling corner and decided that someone was waiting for the dumb Black boy who handed weed to a cop to break.

I went through the list that I sometimes recited when I wondered if I'd arrived at rock bottom. You could have died as soon as you were born. Even your lungs were not ready to move life into your body. Your father died horribly and you fear that you may die in the same way too. You loved your stepfather and can't shake the image of him crying in his prison cell out of your head. There was the Christmas two years ago where you, your brother, and your mom sat in the basement awaiting any kind of news. Dennis had tried to sneak back into the United States but had a heart attack while in police custody. Was he dead?

It took a moment for me to recognize the sensation. Mainly because I'd fought to feel it my entire life and could never muster it. The ball of heat formed in the pit of my stomach first, then spread to my back and up to my spine. In an instant, my birth father, Prince, materialized next to me. His gaze felt as real as the salt water of the Atlantic Ocean hitting the back of my throat. I fell into him.

He talked and talked, knowing that I didn't want too many of my own words filling my head. He told me what he ate for lunch as a kid and how good his mother's cornmeal porridge was. I laughed and agreed. He hadn't gone to prom, but instead, trekked to the United States and stayed up late with my mother in her bedroom as the snow fell heavy outside. He liked "real tough reggae music, di bad bwoy ting go rough." He never imagined having a son that graduated college, traveled the world, and stood up for what he believed in.

"I'm proud of you no matter what. Don't let them break you."

As I waited for hours, I decided that a memory I could give myself, although somewhat untrue, meant more than cheap anecdotes anyone else could try to instill in me about my parents. I slept. I pressed my ear against the metal door and listened for Emma's voice whenever I heard footsteps. Eventually, I was released with a paper in hand that read what felt like my charges, scrawled in red ink—go home, nigger. Listen to your mother. I realized one thing about my arrest. Maybe my father's absence could save me, if I could determine for myself some part of what his absence meant.

The march out of the police department's holding-cell area led me to the top of a stairwell. At the bottom, Emma turned around and smiled at me. We hugged and laughed as we nibbled on chicken in the car.

"Shit, I got out before you?" she cracked.

In the delirium, I was aware that we were laughing at the absurdity of it, having survived something so big and small at the same time. It wasn't until the rest of the group went to sleep, tipsy from beer, that I went to the bathroom and locked the door behind me. Once on the floor, I let the wall of water cover my vision and crash down on me, like a shockwave. Was it fair that I had escaped this hell and my father hadn't? Was it inevitable that his well would find me too?

The reaction from my friends when I got back to Ohio was a mix of amusement and dismay. I couldn't really pull the blinds up and talk to anyone about how utterly humiliated I felt. Even when people asked if I was bitter, I was incapable of blaming any of it on Emma. Capitalism's political violence was to blame.

"Things happen," I usually replied. The truth was that I loved Emma too much to be angry. I simply wanted us to continue fighting and being a political family.

I watched as Emma argued with her mother on the phone about her own arrest. Her car was warm and small as she cried afterward. I decided that most parents had strange ways of navigating the fear that the world would kill their children, even if their fear sometimes pushed their children away, mutilated them into the things that they feared the most.

I didn't like loud, abrupt sounds as much anymore. I'd look out at Court Street as people ducked in and out of bars, laughing with their friends. Over cranberry vodkas at a sticky bar, Emma, Angela, and I drew the same conclusion. Nothing else felt as important anymore. For weeks, I could lose focus and be right back on the highway, watching the horse kick its massive legs into the air as I waited for its hooves to smash my teeth, break my cheekbones, and explode my eyes into my melting head. If you searched for America or asked the hard questions, America could rear its sun-bleached head, a forever duppy playing God and plotting death.

Maybe this duppy of death was brought on by *Revolutionary Suicide*. Or all of the blushing, white faces staring back at me as the cop led me out of the Bill Clinton rally. Or the Indigenous man staring me down, demanding that I take off my jacket. But mostly, it was what I had conjured when I had my father talk to me. I had moved the stone from the cave's entrance, squandered the last of my illusions, and made too many bets. The dam and its waters, filled with the reminders of mortality, were rushing toward me.

"This country is going to kill me," I said to a friend at a bar after my fifth drink. "And what a horrible death that would be. "

...

I returned to Standing Rock one last time. Emma and I attended our court dates. I wore my jacket inside the courtroom, but sweated the whole time. I plead guilty, avoided any jail time, and got fifty dollars back from the bail that my friends had raised on my behalf. Emma screamed "Fuck 12" as we left.

A few days later, I stood in Sacred Stone Camp in shock as I stared at the news on my phone. Donald Trump was president-elect.

"You need a hug?" said two Indigenous men as I passed them. I sensed a deep recognition in their gazes and hugged them. I called my mother and lied about where I was.

"Why did I become a citizen for this?" she asked. I had no answer for her.

In my mind's eye, there are three moments that define the end of Standing Rock for me. There was the night when Emma wandered off to meet up with other camp acquaintances that she was particularly tight-lipped about, once again yielding her stoicism. Then two other people I knew vanished from my camp. Then miles into the distance, but still visible in the moonlight, a patch of land was set ablaze.

"The pipeline?" Someone near me guessed.

I watched, both terrified and caught like a dog staring at something dangerous but beautiful. The dangerous and beautiful thing was how the orb of orange and red cut through the otherwise blue night and set off a sort of sunrise.

I would be far away in another country by the time that Oceti Sakowin was raided and burned for the last time. As the movement dissolved physically, a memory of a morning there came to mind. Crawling through a field of thick mud, avoiding camp security, and sneaking to a meeting location for an action, which was canceled. My friends and I were tired and hungry, but somewhat relieved. Emma stood next to me, her hair sticking up in patches. We exchanged a glance, a knowing that small moments can define an entire chapter of our lives, a tattoo of sorts like the one etched on both of our bodies.

"It means you can be both soft and hard at the same time," Emma once explained when asked about the tattoo.

For weeks, snow and blizzards ravaged everyone who stayed devoted to the movement until the end. Donald Trump became president in January 2017 and riots tore through the United States. White people went wild at the notion that America was ending, or at least, taking a dark turn. Black and brown people were going about our lives, confronting our reality through a different, more personal kind of grieving, or simply putting the work in to live beyond the America laid out for us.

One image from the February 2017 raid of Oceti Sakowin stopped me in my tracks. It was of an Indigenous man, aged twenty-two, as he stood in front of a pile of burning wood and tents. He wore a dark beanie that covered shoulder-length black hair. His face was somber, yet strong as he stared at the camera. His name was Chanse. Samantha and I met him our first week there. We thought that he was cute and said hello to him any chance that we got. He had dropped everything, like so many others, to join the movement. Unlike so many others, he had stayed until the end and would go on to do more.

On a November evening after my last time in Standing Rock, I caved, called Whitney, and asked to contact her friend, who was a medium, that she'd mentioned in the car. On the phone, the medium was calm as he told me that he could see my father standing in his backyard, dressed in some kind of Cherokee garb.

I felt a lump in my throat as the medium said, "Your father is coming through to me. He says that you're the apple of his eye."

Minutes later, I hung up the phone, unable to remove the same lump in my throat that had emerged when Whitney had tried to pass her platitudes on to me in the car about how my birth father loved me from some place in the sky. When things end, especially in violent ways, it becomes the job of those left behind to decide what survives and what is forgotten. Curiosity becomes both a path to truth and danger.

I decided, despite everything, that something about Chanse's gaze in the Standing Rock photo, strong and unrelenting as everything precious burned behind him, gave me hope. His willingness to stay and live in a reality with others, no matter how soul affirming or breaking, gave me hope. To stay and live with others, even if it meant death. In a way, it felt like Chanse had gone on a journey parallel to my own, a journey steeped in staring death down and saving himself anyway, despite the chill of its reach.

Paris, France, and Fez, Morocco, 2018

The breeze was cool as we settled in our chairs outside of the hotel's front doors. My aunt smoothed out her yellow dress and fixed her sunglasses. We spent the afternoon roaming around Montmartre looking for lunch. My aunt cackled over her pronunciation of the menu items and my mouth watered as soon as the French onion soup arrived. At Sacré-Cœur, we bought Heineken beers out of a man's cooler and watched the other tourists. I was happy to be with her since she was the first family member to ever visit me during a trip abroad.

"More wine?" my aunt asked.

After the Philippines, I moved to Cleveland, the city that I had grown up in, and lived with my mother. During my year at home, I noticed how drastically Cleveland had changed. When I was a senior in high school, the Flats was the neighborhood that people raised their eyebrows at when I told them my high school prom was there. Now it had expensive high-rise apartments and breweries with white yuppies threatening to call the police on Black homeless people. I studied more about Cleveland history. In 1968, Black militants engaged in a shootout with Cleveland police in Glenville. I realized that taking our history seriously and the fact that we are a part of shaping it is important. If we don't engage with and protect our history, it will be mutilated or erased.

I struggled through my first bouts of freelance writing and fantasized about joining a movement somewhere else in the country. I went to San Francisco with Nadia and my brother to receive a grant for my media work. After a party there with three open bars, my brother stopped me on the sidewalk outside, shook my shoulders too hard, and told me he was proud of me. Though the moment felt nice, some part of me didn't believe him. How do you know enough about my life to even be proud of me, I thought. I drank copious amounts of red wine with my friend Kim when I returned to Cleveland. One night after an upsetting phone call with Eli, I sulked outside of a bar with her. Feeling like my life was once again wandering away from me, I said, "Everything is changing."

By spring of 2018, I was convinced that I needed another big adventure. I resolved to turn twenty-four years old on holy ground. I wanted to follow the tradition of bold and gay Black men. Greatness, to me, equated to understanding the significance of the small and grandiose choices that we make. My summer in France would mark seven decades since James Baldwin had run off to the city, moved into a hotel, and battled his heaviness abroad. His adventure had been to find literary stardom, love, and fame.

The day of my flight, I called Angela and couldn't stop crying as I packed my bags. The immensity of my own decision snuck up on me at the last moment. I imagined going to

France, feeling awkward and trapped for committing myself to three months there with friends I hadn't seen in two years. I wasn't the right person to be doing any of this. My mother came home from work. With her hand to her chest, she said, "I knew something was different in your voice when you called me. I could tell."

After my first visit to France, Enzo came to the United States and spent time with me. My wayward romance wandered with me in Ohio and I played with the idea of three months in France. Great decisions lead to hurricanes of change and growth. Do it now or you never will, I thought.

This trip felt more like being a part of Enzo's community. Now when I entered spaces, I was either the American or the boy that made Enzo light up. Shortly after arriving, Enzo wrapped his hand around my lower back and stopped me outside of his house. He tried to bury the shyness in his expression and said, "My friend is leaving her apartment for a few days. I would like to stay there with you alone, if that is okay with you?"

I nodded, stunned. Enzo smiled, then kissed me in the daylight. I still liked that he wore scarves like every Frenchman that I saw in movies, how he wiggled his small butt when he cooked and listened to music, and the deep place that his laughter originated from, especially when he looked at me. His gaze was unnerving.

On our first night, he cooked pasta with tomato sauce, then kissed me deeply as we fell into his friend's bed. With the window open, Enzo fell asleep with his head resting in my lap. I stared out the window, listened to Cigarettes after Sex, and tried to quantify what I was so afraid of.

"I just don't know if I'm doing a dumb thing here," I confessed to Kevin at a party after my first few nights of staying with Enzo.

Kevin was an American friend that ran with some of the same people as I did in France. We met on a couch at a college party. I listened for a long time as he brushed his blond hair behind his ear and talked about the uninspiring nature of his film program. He was usually stoic, which could make me nervous, but also forced me to calm myself sometimes in his presence. To me, he seemed more existentially sure of himself than I could ever be, or at least, he put on a measured face.

We were at a party during one of my first nights back in France. People danced shirtless and sipped cold beers from the fridge. I'd had wine and molly and puffs of weed before kissing a man that went up to every guy at the party before saying, "I'm trying to break a record for the number of kisses in one night. Would it be okay if I kiss you?"

I kissed the man with force and tried to make him stay with my lips. A half an hour later, the molly took hold of my body and made Kevin look young and wise as we cornered each other outside. I was mesmerized as he leaned in close, looked at me darkly, then said, "You just have to fucking go for it, right? You can't hold back. All of this shit that capitalism and this fucked-up world puts on us, throw it away. Love is the only currency that we have when all this shit falls. Defend it. Go for it. How could you do anything else?"

It all sounded grand coming out of his mouth, but despite all my musings and longings for love, to have it staring at me in the face was terrifying. When I was younger and often begged for a gift, if my father bought it for me and presented it in a sentimental way, I froze. I'd somehow already detected a glimpse of something—the performativity and role-playing that was coded into so many relationships. Some adults tell lies or the same stories and expect their children to follow along and believe their version of reality. Children become the puzzle piece to be picked up by their parents and sorted into the right place, to fit their narrative. What disjointed me about the concept of motherhood was that I was expected to love and reshape parts of myself because my mother had given me the gift of life. For fatherhood, the mystery was being told to be strong by men that were so largely defined by their absence, their form of exodus. Being away made me aware of growing up with these expectations and how I wanted them to no longer control me.

I drank more wine after Kevin's pep talk in a kind of panic. More intoxicated now, I found Enzo and pulled him aside to talk. Somehow the conversation drifted to my mother. I buried my face into Enzo's chest. A red light bulb cast down on us. My fear grew fangs and dug into me. I couldn't play the wholly confident new lover. The ruptures in my life were expanding and fusing together. I started to cry about my father, the dead one, and my other father, the deported one. A part of me opened more suddenly than I expected when I didn't work as hard to appear so strong to Enzo.

"You can tell me anything," Enzo purred as he ran his hands through my hair.

Until then I understood love skewed, the love imbued in queer friendship, a love that a collective politic could unravel, but not a romantic love. To me, self-love was owning my independence. Now I had to navigate how my body and mind moved in romance. This challenge terrified me. I tried to will myself to James Baldwin's truth, "Love takes off masks that we fear we cannot live without and know we cannot live within."

Shortly after, May Day, which was also known as International Worker's Day, occurred. I went out to the demonstrations with Enzo and Kevin. After an hour or so of seemingly aimless marching, a nearby McDonald's had bricks thrown through its windows and was set on fire. Police surged toward the crowd and set off flash grenades that shot off small pieces of shrapnel. A bottleneck formed and people ran across a bridge, cheering on other demonstrators that chased off police alongside the Seine. We wandered into a nearby occupation of a university building. While going for a drink of water, I heard screaming as people tried to close a large metal door that had been locked to stop random outsiders from entering the courtyard. I leapt forward and struggled to help push the door closed. In an instant, an arm shot out and sprayed me at close range with pepper spray. The evening darkened. I walked away with my face feeling like a molten lava field.

The more that I engaged with French people, the more I could begin to navigate the drastic differences between their lives as Europeans and mine as a Black man in an anti-Black world, and the political challenges that I faced. I wanted to begin to find a language to speak to the specificity of how the world tried to destroy me and how this violence, which hangs over every Black person's head like a guillotine before we are even born, can inform and influence a revolutionary practice. For me and many other radicalized, young Black people, a revolutionary outlook was necessary to grasp our autonomy, to define our history, and to uncoil our anger in the present moment.

This is what I loved about the image of Nina Simone and James Baldwin, smiling as their heads leaned against each other's or as they frolicked to music. Or Nikki Giovanni exposing him on his consistent erasure of Black women. Or the thought of Jimmy in a diner booth with his best friend, Eugene Worth, in 1946. The two are disagreeing about dark and deep political shit, the kind of shit that breaks you open in front of the people that you love the most, and sometimes you must face that fact that they can't stitch you back together and tell you what you need to hear. Shortly after that conversation, Worth jumped to his death from the George Washington Bridge. His absence would loom over Baldwin's life creatively, existentially, and romantically. All of the scenes meant that we must take the suffering with the good in order to be great.

Although I revered Baldwin, I didn't want the same life as he had. Our configurations of imperfection were different. I wanted to be seen and I didn't want to be dependent upon one person for that. I didn't revere his fantasies about America being the mother we have to return to in order to make better. Why should I love the America that helped upend my parents' island and wanted to see me rot in a cage? What freedom did suckling that breast give me? What sustenance instead of poison?

If America could not deliver me what I deserved as a young and curious Black person, I deserved to try to find it where I could and not be overpowered by the kind of son or citizen I needed to be. This mentality was why Peter Gelderloos wrote, "And the best parts of our lives are anarchy already!"

There was a boy in the neighborhood that I'd always notice riding his bicycle around. Red coat flapping behind him. His slight curls falling down his pale cheeks. Angular expression. It was nearing the end of my first month in France when I went to a birthday party with a friend. A table near the window was filled with liquor, so I poured heavy drinks. Techno music filled the air. I looked over the dance floor and noticed people periodically hugging the boy with the red jacket. I realized that the party was for him. With my limbs loosened by the alcohol, I danced with my friend and when the birthday boy found me, he smiled.

"Enchanté. My name is Leo."

By the end of the night, Leo and I found our hands on each other, groins grinding, and my tongue in his mouth as his partner stood a few feet away. Weeks later, I ran into Leo again at a book reading in someone's backyard. He invited me back to his apartment filled with moving boxes. In such a short time, I had already witnessed his life-changing shape.

"We can read some poetry in my room," Leo said, slender in the doorway, as his friends slinked off to bed.

In his room were white walls, more boxes, and lots of books. We sat on his bed, leafed through poems and glanced at each other. Leo started to read his poetry. Then said, "You know, I wrote a poem about you when we met."

Eventually I laid back on his bed. His lips caressed mine. In the brightly lit room, we kissed and pressed and pushed against each other. I wanted his passion to swallow my passion. He hushed and reminded me that we should stay silent.

"The walls are thin."

I loved that my fingers could be inside of him as his muscles exploded. He gripped my wrist, slackened against my arm, and sweat next to me. Leo asked if Enzo and I were together. I stared up at the white ceiling and told Leo that Enzo and I hadn't defined our relationship at all yet.

"When I'm with my partner, we're very open about sex and what we want. It has taught me a lot," Leo said. "You are only the second guy I've ever been with."

As opposed to other bicurious men I'd had flings with, Leo was confident, equipped even as I noticed the bottle of poppers on his bedside. In my experience, it had been rare for a newly bicurious man to have the confidence to tug your wrist to move your finger deeper inside of his body, to relax enough to find pleasure in the act. I liked Leo because he represented a vision that filled me with warmth. I was no longer the boy in the corner waiting to be seen or loved. I was a man that could be loved and navigate other pleasures too.

I told Enzo about my night with Leo right away. In the warm light of his bedroom, Enzo nodded, shrugged coolly, and muttered, "That's not surprising. I had a feeling there was something between you two."

It was later that he sat me down again and told me he hadn't been fully honest, that he had been a bit jealous, not because I had "done anything wrong" but instead because he was realizing how much he felt for me.

"Sometimes you just seem so prepared on what you want to say."

I tried to decipher what Enzo was saying. We decided that our relationship could be open. The more I thought of his perception of me, the more I realized that growing up in an environment where so many drastic changes were never brazenly confronted or processed in my presence had affected me. A gay Black boy could be told to hold his tongue and be made invisible for the parts of himself that would eventually force him to see so much of the world. Queer Black people quite literally create new words out of the space that we share with each other, and our appreciation of their power helps us create stories.

After the party where I opened up to Enzo, I arranged for friends to visit me during my May and July in France. Alex, a college friend, was among the first friends to arrive in May. We followed Enzo's crowd to the countryside. We piled ourselves under blankets in the attic of the brick house that had a window overlooking the front yard of flowers. There was no internet. I begrudged myself for not bringing more books. We ate lentils and rice for dinner while drinking stolen wine. I butchered my French. Every morning, Alex and I had the ritual of staring out at the cows in the field across the street as we yelled, "OÙ EST LES VACHES?" In the nearest town, we strolled around while looking for pharmacies through the cramped streets and drank cold beers as a church bell rang in the distance.

Three more friends arrived shortly after Alex. We flew to Barcelona, helped clean out a newly squatted apartment, drank vodka by the water, and skirted around the travel tensions brewing among us. Most of June was spent doing random trips to other cities, smoking weed in small trailer homes, feeling like the main character in *The Dreamers*, and softly falling asleep in Enzo's bed as he kissed me goodbye while I listened to the audiobook of *Call Me By Your Name*. He usually went off to work or ran errands. The reach of Aciman's book moved my organs to different parts of my body. My heart to my throat being the most important. I had never read a writer that could dive into the psychology of love so vividly. I related to Elio's neglectful, then overpowering longing.

At a party at Enzo's house, I found myself looking at him in the way Elio had in the film adaption of *Call Me By Your Name* during their last drunken night together—woozy, a little lost, a lot found, and more than willing to be gazed back at. I pressed him against the wall, kissed him, and stared at him. How had I ended up here? Was this whole thing changing me? Hadn't I wanted to be changed by love all along? In his room as the music blasted on the first floor, he peeled off my clothes, then breathed the words "I love you" heavy into my ear. I had decided what my reaction would be earlier when I tried to fold him into my memory permanently, so I said the same back immediately.

It was glorious to be living out my own iteration of Elio's words, especially from the section near the end of the novel where he begins "to take mental snapshots of him [Oliver], picked up the bread crumbs that fell off our table and collected them for my hideaway, and, to my shame, drew lists." My list involved my body inside his body and watching his back tense in the dark, his slow saunter in his underwear to the bathroom, how he found me in bed, sometimes looked over my shoulder as I wrote, or snuck his hand around my waist beneath my jacket. Most of all was the thought that kept pounding in my mind, "You'll never be as young as you are in this moment.

Fuck and love with splendor." It was a push through an open door, which I was also perpetually terrified would eventually close.

In a park one day shortly after we said we loved each other, Enzo stared at me, then said, "I just want you to know that there are parts of you that I don't understand, but I love you so much."

He left and I drank beer in the sunlight. My mind tumbled around itself, trying to make sense of his words in the way that people in relationships with different native languages do. Was he saying that I wasn't open? Or that he imagined there were parts of me that scared him? Were there parts of me that he hadn't found yet that he anticipated he may love even more than what I'd been capable of showing him? His introspection tunneled my mind.

June 30 marked the end of my second month in France and my birthday, which aligned with the birthdays of two other friends in the city. After cake, wine, liquor, finger foods, and gifts, we danced in their cleared dining room. I dangled onto Enzo and teased him playfully for playing too much Britney Spears. Leo arrived. We suckled each other's necks in an empty room. I felt his dick through his pants. Leo and Enzo danced. I twirled with Leo's partner. In an entirely new and primordial way, I realized that I'd arrived to the exact place I'd always wanted to be—in someone else's world smiling with their friends, making memories with them, and realizing that it all really was just the process of falling in love. And falling in love proved to be a brave thing, one of the first life decisions that fully felt like mine.

I might move past this story that I've had for myself, I thought. I can move to France and be more human. Maybe my aunt visiting tomorrow will not care when I tell her I am gay.

By the end of the night, the floor was sticky with beer, and the party cleared. I trailed behind Enzo to his room, holding his hand the whole time. In his bedroom, we laid next to the open window. I closed my eyes and he held me. His warmth, which had anointed the entire day with safety, helped me realize that the adventure had changed. I had stumbled upon another home away from home, another place to rest my head. The dream in the back seat before Standing Rock, the paralyzing silence around my father's murder, the ice scraper held high by my mother, the dull thud on my brother's face as the scraper struck his coat, and the theater of being a Black body abroad; all of it was very far away.

I wasn't living out this experience for Baldwin anymore. I had stolen something from his iteration of freedom. Baldwin had crafted a blueprint and now I was crafting my own.

■ ■ ■

The days are mixed or I mix them in my head to make it easier. My aunt arrives in France. It is a long walk to her hotel. She hugs me warmly in her dim room where the blinds are shut. We take the train to Montmartre. I tell her stories about that spring and things about travel that I have never told other family members. When she meets Enzo, she squeals with excitement and hugs him fiercely. I have to clutch at my chest to keep my heart from trying to jump out of it. Walking through

Versailles Palace, Enzo holds my hand. My aunt laughs, her yellow dress fluttering in the breeze and sunlight. We eat ice cream and return to Paris on the train. My aunt takes photos of Enzo and me constantly. Her camera's lens becomes God's eyes. God's eyes are glistering down on us.

Enzo must go home, so I stay with my aunt. I am happy to finally be sharing this part of my world with someone who has known me my entire life.

After three glasses of wine and long conversation, she stares at me and speaks, "There's a lot you don't know about your father's death." She sighs, then continues, "Honestly, the truth might make you hate a lot of people."

"The truth?"

I try to study her face, but it is already shaded. We are already walking back to her hotel room. I remember to breathe in between steps, to not let the storm in my stomach reach my shielded expression.

An hour later, my aunt is sleeping in her bed. I am holding myself so tightly that it feels like I may crush my own body. It is the only way to cry as violently as I am while staying almost completely silent. There is snot. My skin glistens like a seal and I think my head may explode. The waves are crashing down. I am diving into Jamaica, all those questions about my father, and the fact that all the silences lead back to the very beginning. My mother's gaze moves through me darkly and toward a memory of her saying, "You laugh just like him sometimes, you know?" The underlying tightness in her tone translates to, "You feel joy just like he did and for that, maybe you can't be forgiven."

I am a child, trailing out of school behind my brother after some nameless bout of emotion has taken me. My brother leers up at me from the bottom of the stairwell in dismay and annoyance. He can't hear the caged bird trying to flutter out of my chest because I can't hear it either. The beating of the bird's wings is a wailing that has followed me my entire life; the same boy on the cement ledge during recess, or the bewildered boy staring back at my grandmother in Jamaica when I am ten. I am crying because I miss my mother, so my grandmother says, her tone like a viper, "Why are you crying? Did someone hurt you? People only cry like that when someone is really hurting them." The same boy in the basement stricken to silence or better yet, flailing out of that water. A Black boy simply finding the justification to scream, even if it could kill him in the water or level a world.

Then I am nineteen years old and fiddling with the radio in my grandmother's attic in Cleveland. She coughs, breathes, and admits that my father left it there while he was in prison.

Again and again and again while in the hotel room with my aunt, I realized the secrets were the silence. The silence brought me into the world. Seven months later, the silence chased my father after he lunged out of the back seat. The silence took Dennis. The silence helped my mother escape her working to know me. The silence took Crystal, but I hoped gave her bliss in whatever realm was next.

In my grandmother's attic as we stared at the silver radio, I realized that it wasn't just America that had tried to condition the silence into me, but it was also my family's trek for survival, which didn't have space for a boy that wanted to know more about his murdered father.

"Prison?" I say.

My grandmother realizes that I did not know. I leave her house and curse myself for not asking to have the radio. I start to believe I can answer the questions. How do you lose something that you never really had? How do you miss someone that causes those who knew him to react to the mention of him with a heavy sigh or fond laughter? Is it too much to hope to resurrect someone with your mind and heart? Do we get punished for playing God?

"Your memory gets in the way of my memory" is what the Kashmiri American poet, Agha Shahid Ali, once wrote. This means that I stumble upon some strange and unexpected truth about my father. That truth gives him weight. The weight, coupled with the silence, becomes unbearable.

I am losing my father. Then I am losing my father. Then on the bathroom floor, I am losing my father and my family all over again as the past meanders and explodes, and for the first time, I can see it differently. I bury the sleeve of my shirt in my mouth and try to text anyone that I can. How can I explain this other than I have explained it before? There is the boy in my second-grade class. He is waving his hands over a dictionary. His eyes roll to the back of his head. He mutters, rolls his eyes forward, and speaks.

"Your father is waiting in the cemetery. He is angry."

I imagine my father's decaying body rising from the dirt. His skin has fallen off in patches. There are sores and boils and wounds. Entire parts of him that have turned to congealed mush. He smells of flesh buried under land and then forgotten. He begins to call out to me. Instead of feeling beckoned to the lighthouse like a lost traveler, I am shaken, rattled by a dead man's lips calling my name. I wonder if I have killed him simply because my life, as long as it stretches, is a direct measurement of his death. His anger could be brewing from the dirt, lifting his body from the grave.

For that entire evening after my classmate raised his hands over that dictionary, I contemplate climbing out my bedroom window, dropping down to my front yard, and making the walk to Calvary Cemetery, totally unable to gather the significance of the place I imagined wandering to to see my father. Calvary is defined as "an experience of extreme suffering."

If Aunt Vick is correct in what she said to my mother in the hospital about some people having to die so that others can live, then it was me, the product of a violent past, that the silence bothered the most. What horrors had he committed? What did it mean that no one wanted to help me figure them out?

Silence had defined my relationship with my father. It locked him away into a chest. Now I must open the chest with the key, crack the ribs open. This need is why Audre Lorde once wrote that "we fear the visibility without which we cannot truly live."

When they tell you to be good, to be well-mannered, and to follow the rules because this is how America will let you live, they do not tell you that even with your college degree, America will place the barrel of its gun in your tooth-torn mouth, break your back in its car, and feed you to the pigs. We do not survive what we don't even begin to confront. Silences can kill us when we give them too much power. I do not want to be afraid of my father because I did not want to be frozen by the unknown. Especially when it lunges out at me from the universe, trying to wrap itself around me and make me a part of it.

■ ■ ■

It is the summer when I am fifteen years old. My mother and I are at a park gathering for local Jamaicans. I walk around and try to find some soda. A voice that I'd never heard before stops me in my tracks.

"Prince?"

I turn around. A Black woman in her thirties wearing leggings and a purple Aéropostale shirt stands in front of me. She inhales. As she walks toward me, I see the memories moving through her face. Her look never crosses my mother's face, not even when I ask her about my father. Or maybe if I think about it hard, my mind moves to her cold slap across my face that night in the kitchen; how, in some way, that slap was her way of negotiating the past through me.

Around us a circus of kids play on a jungle gym. Women sell jerk chicken out of the trunks of their cars. Stereos are blasting murder music. The woman tells me that she knew my father. He was a kind of father figure to her and she wants to tell me all about him. My heart soars as she writes her number on a piece of paper and departs after saying, "Call me anytime and I'll tell you everything about him."

I tell my mother of this encounter and we drive home in silence. She walks into my room, her posture hard as she leans into the door frame.

"Give me the paper," she says. I balk in the face of her fury and hand it over. She rips it to shreds in front of me, then mutters as she walks away, unaware that something psychic is moving between us. "There are some things that you just can't understand yet."

I wonder about the death certificate that I found in the attic with his name and the list of his injuries on it. I wonder what makes me different, more special, or more punishable than other Black boys. I wonder about coming out to my parents. I wonder if Prince were alive, would he love the real me or beat me into a more unrecognizable mess?

■ ■ ■

The journey back home was grueling. I told Enzo of the impending doom of what I must ask my mother once I return home. I can't stop crying as I talk to him. He wiped my tears and scowled as I said, "I keep wondering how much I can take. What if this is the thing that breaks me?"

During my last week in France, I am caught shoplifting a shaving razor from a grocery store. The security guard wrapped his arms around me from behind. In a back room with a camera pointed at me from the ceiling's corner, I downgraded my French, say that I am innocent, and am let go. Another country has just almost swallowed me up. Shortly after, I hitchhiked with Enzo's roommate to a goat farm in southern France. We stole from gas stations and I notice we get rides much more quickly when I go to the bathroom and am not with Enzo's roommate when she asks for rides. For a moment, I wondered how many times I, a Black boy, must practice disappearing before I actually disappear and what a twisted gift that would be in a world mutilated by white supremacy. At the train station while waiting for Enzo, his roommate looked at me and smiled.

"Do you love him?"

I nod.

"I think he's a little afraid."

"Afraid of what?" I said.

"He's never been in love before."

We drove to the goat farm at night. Everything in my life thus far had led me here. It was dark. People danced messily to Britney Spears under a circus tent. I played with the big black dog that belongs to the farm owners, smoked weed, and decided to talk to Enzo. The countryside dirt and air surround us as we sat on a bale of hay. I felt his warmth and looked at him. He was too nervous to stare back.

"What do you want to do when I leave? We've never talked about it."

"I don't know if I should say this, but . . ." he sighed, then said it anyway. "I know that I'm in love with you and I don't care if we have to have an open relationship. I want to make this work however we can."

Before I registered what he'd said, we are kissing. The next day we walked to a nearby lake. I savored the sunlight on my skin. I snapped film photos. And just like that, it was time to leave. At the airport, Enzo cradled my head. He wiped my tears away. The largeness of it smashed down on my chest, ears, and heart. I cried and cried and Enzo held my face, his black eyebrows pressing together. All the while, he never looked away.

"Why are you crying?" he asked.

Suddenly there is no more time, so I tell him what I can, but what I can't tell him about are all those nights sleeping next to Eli in his bed, staring on longingly at parties, kneeling in backyards in desperation to pray to a God I seldom believed in for serenity, and resigning myself to the fact that maybe my soul was just too hot for any one person to hold. I think of the boy standing in front of his mother's truck in his high school parking lot, how he and I could be destroyed in very similar and different ways, and how he couldn't have imagined this very moment.

"Because I'm here with you," I say.

I am already boarding the plane, already moving away from him, staring down at the clouds, and onto the next heavy thing. I can't shake the heat in Morocco or my aunt's words lurking around in my head. This is not a confession without the specifics. It is a secret that I have been born with, will be buried with, or had already been buried with. For weeks, I drink cheap wine from plastic bottles. When the liquid hits too much, I have to leave the cackling guests, stare out at the biggest Medina in the world, and level with myself because all paths have led me here. I meet an Australian woman named Kobi and we become quick friends. We take long train rides through the desert and try not to melt when the train is stuck and our windows can't open. While telling her about my life, I freeze and want to fall apart all over again. I am all the way across the world and I can only talk about my father. I have been worried my whole life that I will never move beyond his story or that my life will just be a strange retelling of his. I had, after all, taken his name as my own during a sunny morning in Standing Rock while reading about a Black man, a father, living out his years in prison.

A confession with the specifics. I bring myself to the precipice and look too far over the edge. The duppy is staring back, lifting its long fingers to its mouth, and pulling at the purple stitches. Blood and skin bounce toward me. America, no, the world is repeating itself. I am afraid my body can't stop the tape from replaying. I have been broken in so many places and the story begins to crawl inside the cracks until it fills me. Becomes me.

I am sitting on the couch in my mother's basement. I turn to her and ask the question that I have always wanted to ask. She looks at me. A veil of acceptance cloaks her expression. She starts speaking, and for the first time, someone other than my father begins to take shape.

"You had an uncle. His name was Cedric. They called him Doggie. You met his daughter once when you were fifteen."

Montego Bay, Jamaica, 1962–2010

I learned that Cedric Murray grew up in Montego Bay. He was born in 1973, the same year the United States sent its secretary of state to Jamaica to dissuade the island's relationship with Cuba. By the time Cedric could speak, the island's political wars continued. Gangsters sped away from 56 Hope Lane and toward Tivoli Gardens, a Jamaica Labour Party stronghold, with the tires of their car spinning after Bob Marley's 1976 attempted assassination. Lester "Jim Brown" Coke, the leader of the Shower Posse, was rumored to be among the gunmen.

While speaking with a *Jamaica Gleaner* journalist during the height of Cedric's murder spree, Cedric's former gym teacher chose to remain anonymous for his safety. In his interview, he described Cedric as a quiet kid during the two years that he taught him. Cedric acquired his nickname "Doggie" while in school. These were the same two years that Cedric notes joining the Renegades in his diary. His PE teacher, pen named Fernando Archer, knew that Cedric grew up poor and had parents that put effort into his appearance. He observed that Cedric often sat alone and read comic books about cowboys, a harkening to the last shots of *The Harder They Come* when Jimmy Cliff is shot up on a beach, marking the end for this isolated gangster intercut with shots of moviegoers laughing. Masculine violence is both propagandized and celebrated through media, and inherited through bloodline and culture.

By the mid 1980s, my father, Prince, came to the United States and, like so many other Jamaican men, resorted to drug dealing to earn money to pay the bills and make ends meet for his family. His silver radio was left in my grandmother's attic, a constant ringing that marked his absence. Back in Jamaica, Cedric joined the Renegades in a war against the Piranhas, a rival gang in the St. James area. Once Doggie graduated high school, he fled to the US.

In the Jamaica that Cedric left behind once he moved to the United States, the Shower Posse gang rose to significance. Lester Coke, who grew up in the area that would become Tivoli Gardens, joined the gang lifestyle in 1966 when he was struck six times during a shootout. After recovering from his injuries, Coke went on to control Tivoli Garden in the 1970s. In 1984, he moved the gang's mode of operations to Florida.

The early 1990s marked seismic shifts for all of these men. Cedric, fresh out of high school, and my father, after being deported to Jamaica following his US imprisonment, returned to the Unites States. Coke had a thick CIA file that detailed dozens of murders he was responsible for. In 1992, the United States pressured Jamaica to extradite Coke, who had fled back to Tivoli Gardens, where he now represented a Robin Hood figure that could punish rapists and help the poor pay their bills. When Coke was arrested, he said to a cellmate, "is not

I-one going down alone." Just days before his extradition to the US in February 1992, Lester Coke was burned alive in his jail cell. Now without a father, Christopher "Dudus" Coke took over the Shower Posse at the age of twenty-three.

In 1994, I was born. On February 11, 1995, my father went on a trip with a few acquaintances to Florida. Before leaving, he called a friend and mentioned the outing. I imagine his voice was sweet and calm as he wished this childhood friend a happy birthday. Then he climbed into the car, which was maybe brown and rickety, as the snow fell in layers outside. Partway through the journey and somewhere in West Virginia, a scuffle broke out in the back seat. My father, a fit man following his exercising in prison, fought hard. He pelted his attackers with his fists until his knuckles scraped and bled. Then he opened the door, hit the pavement, and sprinted for his life before he was shot down.

At the center of my gravity is this moment. It is the earliest part of my life that involved death without any kind of heroism. It was the first wound that ripped me open and never quite healed. My father's murder, like some seed at a young age, convinced me of the James Baldwin quote, "Not everything that is faced can be changed, but nothing can be changed until it is faced." To me this meant one of the ways that the old can be accountable to the young is by telling them the truth, which requires the old to face the horrible things about the world that they wish to change. When our elders turn away from this choice, we are all left spinning on hamster wheels of illusion. We don't get to know if someone we loved died cold, scared, or strangely relieved. The illusion becomes the truth.

The more I moved through my life, the more my father's absence followed me. Even in my dreams, I found him. In one, I am darting through a hospital maze as large men chase me down. Everything is bright and he appears suddenly as I turn a corner. The paternal, ravenous shock in his expression almost knocks me over. He grabs my arms and speaks with the force of all the bodies decayed at the bottom of the Atlantic. He says, "Run." We depart from each other, like ghosts running toward the end of oblivion.

In another dream, I am at a phone booth when I am shot down. There is no pain, only engorged panic, as I fall over. In my last moments, I am bleeding out, crawling toward the phone, crawling toward infinity like my father may have while sprawled out on that front lawn in February 1995. Even in my dreams, death cannot escape us.

Cedric went on to be a prized member of the Stone Crusher Gang, aiding in contract murders across the island and gaining the attention of Jamaican officials in 2006 when his activities helped bring the island's number of homicides to an all-time high. Cedric was among the killers that would take jobs that earned anywhere from a few hundred dollars to thousands of dollars. Cedric, navigating with a particular ethic unlike many of his counterparts, never took jobs that involved the murder of women or children.

The weight of Cedric's participation in the 2006 triple murder of my uncles, Senel and Derrick, and one of their girl-friends cannot be understated. These murders also ironically put Cedric on the police's map. When I first Googled Cedric, I skimmed past his photo and ignored the text behind the mug shot. I finally noticed the text and read it in a whisper. Past Cedric's dark skin and curious gaze read "wanted in connection with triple murder." Maybe the writings are always on the walls. We just need the right kind of vision to focus on them.

In January 2008, Cedric helped defend Eldon Calvert, the Stone Crusher Gang leader who was wanted for murder charges, against the police's attempt to apprehend him during Operation Kingfish. Cedric called a friend of his that day and told him that he loved him and that he didn't think he would survive the raid. Cedric was gathered with friends and gangsters in an apartment with a cache of weapons. Raids on Tivoli Gardens had a history of involving violent clashes with the police. Gangsters saw the police's hope of entering Tivoli Gardens unscathed as a pipe dream. So Cedric hid out, shot for his life, and narrowly escaped with Calvert, who was wanted for over a dozen grisly murders on the island.

Five alleged gunmen and two police officers were killed. Cedric later told a friend that numerous young men sacrificed themselves to allow him to get out. Shortly after, Calvert was arrested and charged on drug crimes.

In all of my visits to Jamaica, my family worked as hard as possible to shield me from the violence there. I was safe and taken care of. During an outing to the movies with Tomita when I was nine, my aunt picked us up from the theater halfway through the showing. She drove us home in a panic and told us to crouch down in the back seat. I imagined large Black hands with guns yanking us out of the seats and beating us in the street. I now wonder if Cedric was a part of the outside havoc my aunt wanted to save us from.

"We were there to see how fiction was made," writes Frank B. Wilderson III in *Afropessimism*, "not what fiction meant or whose lives it enhanced or how it greased the wheels of death for others."

In my searching to learn more of my father and his brother, Cedric Murray, I found Wilderson's words to be true. If I could fold the trajectory of my father's life over my own, various ghosts are resurrected. Various truths about manhood, trauma, and healing are found. What fictions had I inherited? And could they destroy me before I knew of their existence?

By thirteen, Cedric would watch his brother, Prince, go off to prison in the United States and he'd join the Renegades. By the time I reached the same age, I'd already helped polish and shine Dennis's hideaway apartment, terrified of whatever beast was swelling inside of me. Uncle Senel wished to tell me about the existence of Cedric Murray, a man I had yet to know existed. Uncle Senel was dissuaded from telling me the truth. In February 2006, he was killed by the very man he wanted to expose to me.

On May 23, 2010, Cedric was in Tivoli Gardens while police raided in order to extradite Christopher Coke. On this night, a Kingston police precinct burned. Police, angered by this act, rushed into people's homes and ordered young men into the streets. Many residents speak of scenes that harken back to past state-sanctioned atrocities, like the Green Bay Massacre—young men ordered out of their homes and killed by police in the streets, and families forced to hide for days as police completed their operation of revenge. Cedric fired his AK-47 until his fingers went numb and he ate gunpowder.

He narrowly escaped, a father of numerous children with a tumultuous love.

At the same time, I was a world away in Ohio. I may have noticed a headline or two about the operation in Jamaica. It would have passed my adolescent brain without a scratch on the record. On May 27, 2010, my mother shook me awake and asked if I was gay. I wandered into a new world, a new version of myself. The next night, I stood in my school parking lot and wondered if my father thought his life was about to end when he got into that car in February of 1995. I wished that some-one, some adult meant to protect me, would save me. Most of all, some part of me grieved my newly lost life, a life where a straight but dead father could be a model of how to live for his straight Black son in America.

If Cedric and Prince could destroy other people, and my family had the power to destroy me, what hope did any of us even have in finding the wound, assessing the damage, and healing? At what point do I separate their violence from the violence that an authentically queer life unearthed? If you are Black, you are born without a future. You are born with a loaded past of cemetery gates that you must pass through.

By the time he was eighteen in 1991, Cedric would come to United States and start his new life here. Upon graduat-ing high school at seventeen in 2011, I ventured to Kingston to visit Dennis after he was released from prison. Cedric sold drugs and learned to kill. I dared to speak my truth on an island known for casting out, beating up, or murdering people like me.

Our exoduses, although guided by Black or Jamaican mas-culinities, are different. During his time on the run, Cedric must have learned the value of community and the terror of isolation after he aided in the 2006 murder of my uncles, Senel and Derrick. He lived in the bush. He sought refuge in Tivoli Gardens. He bore children and beat his lover when he was angry. As more people were murdered around him, the duppy of death inched closer and closer.

On August 12, 2010, it was Cedric Murray's thirty-seventh birthday when he climbed into a car. As the sun rose and covered the roadsides and brush, Cedric may have pulled out a joint, lit it, and breathed, a rare moment of bliss. Maybe he was planning to see his lover or go on another job or simply find another hiding spot.

A part of me hoped his isolation gave him a vision, a glimpse into a possible future—fleeing to Cuba, like so many politically tied gangsters before him, and buying a house that he and his many kids could grow old in. As the years passed, he would list around them and tell stories of an old life riddled with death. In his new life, he has studied, opened up the many locks covering his chest, and tells his children what it truly means to be good.

A song could have come on the radio that rattled the car and made him smile. Cedric would've reached for the volume and turned it all the way up. Prince Jazzbo's voice was loud. Cedric would remember the heat in that basement club, the glistening and swaying bodies, and his brother's hand holding him, guiding him to the front of the crowd. The song crooned, "Have no fear living in Babylon for Jah gonna show you the way."

Cedric was killed by the Westmoreland police, who riddled his car with bullets and said that he never returned fire. The head of Westmoreland police, Beau Rigabie, found the diary on Cedric's body.

When Black parents tell their Black children to not play with guns outside, it is the tales of men like Cedric Murray that run through their mind. This potential end for her children may be why my mother was so cautious to let me adventure with the Black children in my neighborhood. Black children can only play at being an outlaw or gangster for so long. Soon enough, America or Babylon finds another way to lynch you, ship you off, or shoot you down, like a thirteen-year-old Black boy playing in a park with a toy gun. For Black children, childhood is a short chapter because as James Baldwin says, "It is the innocence that constitutes the crime."

Black adults cannot be innocent to a world always trying to kill them. Black children cannot either. And if they attempt to live beyond the boundaries of the illusion, that does not mean that the violence will not reach them. The violence could kill them before they even register it. The violence sometimes throws a flash grenade into the home and, as the grandmother tries to beat away the flames, the police will shoot the Black child. Black children cannot be innocent because innocence means death. Which means that Black childhood, when our minds are more malleable to the other side, is and can be a walk with death.

For my uncle, Cedric Murray, who went from having cowboy comic books to a Sigpro pistol as his best friend, innocence and madness seems to be what allowed him to move forward, to be volatile toward his partner, to be a God-fearing man, and to be a man with a life so drastically defined by his ability to take others' lives. What was the truth that Cedric was looking for? And did death help him find it?

•••

Cedric would live beyond the years his brother, Prince, did; their lives a strange retelling of each other. Just as Prince's death marked me, Lester Coke's death by smoke inhalation and fire would mark his son, Christopher Coke. It also marked Cedric. Senel and Derrick met their end, huddled in that cement house just thirty or so feet from where I'd sat at the age of ten. My older brother and I, both gay men, are tied by blood, but still stifled by all of the silences.

The questions still remain though. How do we break the cycle? How do we confront the men in our lives for their violences? What happens when we procrastinate this confrontation?

We can create myths or fictions, like Frank B. Wilderson III noted. Or we can do what Dennis did as I sat on his lap as a child as he talked about being born weightless and nationless on that rocking boat. I'd look past him and see the stars, his mother writhing around on that small vessel, and giving birth to screaming life. I think of the gangsters like Christopher Coke who were praised by so many in Tivoli Gardens for his good deeds or how people loved my father so fiercely, despite his rage and active fists.

We can procrastinate these confrontations out of trauma, out of shame, or just out of the desire to leave it all behind. I would be lying if I said it was easy to confront these men while knowing that if they were alive, they could wrinkle their noses in disgust when asked to understand me. However, when we procrastinate these confrontations, we procrastinate the bits of truth that can be discovered and yielded to learn from their mistakes.

"Who am I?" Cedric once asked in his diary.

Later on in his diary, Cedric sort of answers his own question: "But if death should befall me, just remember while you murder me, go home and look at your kids and wonder how perfect are they in an imperfect world. Will your child one day become what I have been accused of? Run along, Mr and Miss perfect because you are just a vampire. You are worse than me."

■ ■ ■

When I think of Cedric's journal and his statements about Babylon, I know that we grow up imperfect in an imperfect world. Although he found solace in his writings, he was unable to fully cope with his reality and deeds. His outlaw past inevitably caught up with him not through imprisonment, but through Babylon and the duppy of death. How could he heal if his outlaw lifestyle and masculinity put him at odds with the very people—family, lovers, and friends—that he could have been accountable to? How could he heal if his superpowers were death and running away? Which is to say, could I heal if my superpowers were life and learning to face it?

When I look at it this way, at his pain this way, the lesson is not about our ability to fantasize about self-actualization. The lesson is, instead, what we are willing to face to actualize the deepest and hidden parts of ourselves.

The following pages are excerpt entries from Cedric Murray's journal. Cedric stated that he hoped to write a book one day to explain his story.

JANUARY 13, 2008

What a day, a day of pure agony and pain and fear and confusion. But by the grace of God it was a great day at the end.
I had life because good prevails over man's evil desire. I have
many rivers to cross and yet still trying to find the hatch.

JANUARY 23, 2008

I sit alone, no friend or woman. I feel like all has gone from me.
I am sad over many things in my life. Its like from January 13,
my quiet life has never been the same . . .

MARCH 19, 2008

I am just a man that's caught up living a gangster life, my movements are restricted. Each day I wonder how will my children
react when they come of age and realize who their dad is . . .

MAY 31, 2009

Long time since I write but life is still with me so it's freedom
from jail, but not my freedom to society that has been stolen.

Better yet my son will born in a few months. That's good and my girl is sweet as ever and she carries my son well. My isolation from society gets farther each year. For now I am at ease but for me things are subject to change any time. I should really write a book but I couldn't be real honest so it wouldn't be a bestseller. Things could be a lot worse so I am thankful for the few. Life is so Full of unsolved mystery and dictators. I long for that real fellowship with others and when will I trust (smile). That's a good one for you. I am a real gangster all out but I love the Lord with a passion. Why I do the things I do? Sin. I can do all things through Christ Who strengthens me. That means I can repent and change but yet my faith is weak. My life is a book of puzzle.

SEPTEMBER 13, 2009

Today I felt a touch of envy in a positive way. I saw a man and his woman going out on a date. I just wish I could just go out with the love of my life, Shanty.

MAY 24, 2010

Invasion of Tivoli Garden by Babylon the enemy, gunshots rang out from every corner of West Kingston and other places of KGN to protect the man Don of all Dons. Christopher Coke, AKA Dudus . . . The man they came after is still free and safe, my Don and friend always. It was a raging gun battle a day I won't forget and such tragedy for Jamaica more than 75 people dies by Babylon, man, baby and woman . . . Because their motive was all wrong. I escape one of the last from where I was under crazy gun fire, but God grace, mercy brought me out untouched and my Don is free. I will always say Jim Brown, I am loyal to the Coke family and my guns will always be ready.

JUNE 22, 2010

Today Christopher Coke-AKA-Dudus AKA-President, was arrested. Some say he was on his way to turn himself in but was sidelined. I am deeply affected but he is still and always will be my Don, I now wonder with both brothers in Jail and TG in a state of confusion whats next with babylon, also can me a wanted man ever returned, who can I trust but still TG, will build back . . .

JULY 25, 2010

This path in the river that I am walking is very rough, along with many mixed up emotions that daily and must Wade. In and still stay positive. Today I am very happy because me and my love, this beautiful Ebony Princess are working things out due to a fall out we had. It's good to smile again, real good. Every man needs a woman. For the last couple days I have been so depress Over my whole life. I now understand why commit suicide. They just give in because the brain just overcrowded in the outlet seems closed.

My life right now is like a jigsaw puzzle with a piece missing. My woman. I am in great distress in agony. I am watching my love life all write apart and can't stop it. When does my pain stop. Well, today is a day, false alarm about Babylon coming. Blank. Running again. It seems like I just can't get in shape. Life in the hills of Saint Andrew is very rough day and night. Babylon is close. Rough movements at times. Loneliness has become my daily companion. I do not want to die but I do not fear death. Mann has decide my fate, but God has the final decision.

JULY 30, 2010

What to do and where to turn? My life a day after my friend, the kid, was killed July 29. I fled so many place of sanctuary which is anywhere I can find. I just be mobile. The kid was a good youth. He just link me up in five minutes he was killed by Babylon.

I realize that I've become immune to death. My emotions has run dry. My present way of life has become very rough. Each day is a tension filled, high alert for me. I miss my kids. I don't know when I'll see them, I am homeless and have many fears.

AUGUST 2, 2010

Wisdom teaches understanding and that means life for the past eight or nine days I've had two different curfew and they have been hard but God grace and mercy will always see me through. My life at times have different levels of tension. I must always learn how to surf on each tension wave. I haven't been able to rest for quite a while but man a real man and yes I am tired in every way. but God is my strength each new day and my rock of direction.

Somewhere near Bullhead City, Arizona, August 10, 2015

I am on my fourth refill of coffee by the time my father arrives
to the diner. It was a slow morning in the hotel room. I turned
the temperature up on my room's AC unit, then went straight
into a shower of scalding water because the shock was needed.
It took me five minutes to put on and tie my shoes. I was nauseated and pushed the scrambled eggs from my continental
breakfast around my plate. I thumbed the photograph of my
father and me as an infant, which was covered with tape to
preserve it, in my pocket.

I was never jarred by having a deadbeat biological father, or
to be more accurate, I never felt unique. America snatches Black
fathers out of our homes, throws them into jail, or hangs them
from trees. What America considers beautiful is fed by Black
pain. The commonality of it gave me something to bond about
with other boys growing up when we got drunk in their garages,
smoked dime bags, and argued with tough love. This intimacy
changed shade in high school when Daquan kissed me on the
mouth while we stood in the bathroom at a friend's party. Then
again when Javion was killed in a shooting on his block.

Daquan loved pussy, but his jovial smiles in my direction sometimes lasted a little long. After gym class, we always happened to shower at the same time. Whenever he put his arm over my shoulder, something in my stomach stirred. We left the bathroom at the party, drank more, and only talked to each other for the rest of the night as everyone else faded into the wallpaper. I couldn't really understand the words that Daquan said, but the spaces between his words told me that he'd loved Ricky, our friend that had gotten locked up earlier that year. By the next week, he and all the other dudes in our grade wouldn't talk to me. I had come out, but not because I'd told anyone. My mouth and the way my body responded to Daquan had said enough. I sometimes wondered if the whole thing had been some cruel test.

"This seat taken?" my father says.

When I turned to look where his voice had come from, my whole chest freezes. He is tall and slim, but not skinny. His black shirt is snug at the bicep. His hair is cut short, but not in a fade. He smells like Aunt Vick, which meant that he smelled like cigarettes. He sits down. I nudge a glass of water toward him, which he doesn't drink right away. He sits with fatigue, then exhales.

I couldn't look away from him and he couldn't look at me for more than a few seconds.

"Did she tell you I was dead?" he asks.

I hate how his accusation against my mother sidesteps the fact that he's done enough wrong for someone to wish him dead. Does he think my mother would lie to protect herself or because it's easier than the truth? Does he believe she has the power to tell everyone around her to lie to me as well? Were they both liars and runaways, like me?

I rest my chin on my hand because it's the only thing that I can do while I was thinking. I stare at him and he finally stares at me back. He has brown eyes and age lines along his forehead. I wonder, Does he get much sleep?

"I kind of thought, or I guess assumed you were dead when I was little. I knew that other kids had dads and I knew that she never really talked about you. Then one Christmas, I just sort of blurted out that you were dead. She came across the room, grabbed me, and was so mad." My mind dizzies as I am brought back to that moment. "It was the first time that she hurt me and I knew it was because of you."

He nods and sips his water when the waitress hands him a menu. He leafs through it and I stare out the window. It perplexed me when I'd finally found where he lived. I never envisioned him living in Arizona. Maybe somewhere more rural, isolated, and quiet that snowed for many months out of the year. Instead it's June. The heat is unbearable and loud, like a marching band getting into a highway accident. Outside, the sun makes everything wavy. I patted my face down three times in the bathroom with a wet rag before he got here and positioned myself near the fan that churned on high above us.

"It's your birthday coming up, right? How old?"

I cross my arms and lean back.

"Twenty-one. I just finished college."

"And you came all the way out here to see me? You're a real one," he says as his eyes light up slightly. "What did you study?"

275

"That's cause you never came to find me," I say back. I search his face, which reveals nothing. So I continue with a sigh, "I studied literature. Writing."

The caffeine tunnels inside of me. I suddenly wanted to leap over the table, grab him by the collar, and scream into his face. Or have him hold me. It doesn't make sense that I am here, that I haven't told my mother or brother that I am here. All I knew is that I'd spent one night making phone calls and checking listings online until I found a photo in a newspaper—he was standing outside at a bar's opening ceremony, shaking some-one's hand and hugging them. I wanted to know why he was smiling so wide in the photograph. I clench my fist in my lap.

"So I have this friend, I had this friend. He was kind of my best friend. We'd do everything together. His mom and my mom had dinner once a week, laughed over wine, and maybe Mom has changed since you knew her, but growing up, I didn't see her light up that often. I didn't see her have that spark and I think maybe that was something you took away or you . . . had a hand in."

If I thought of the best parts of knowing my mother, a few things come to mind: her warm laughter as I brazenly hug her, her penchant for using the cell phone most in the bathroom, and ultimately her undying belief that hard work led to stabil-ity. Maybe she fought the lion and won.

I pause to lick my lips, to check for any reaction in his gaze, which gives nothing away. I keep talking. "And this friend, I knew something was going to happen. I knew the kind of peo-ple he hung out with, not bad people, but people that I knew wanted to use him. I tried to talk to him. I tried to tell my friend, but even when I did, I couldn't say what I needed to say.

I couldn't say, 'Don't do this. Don't kill yourself. There's a whole life ahead with so many things that we can't even imagine right now. Don't mess it up.'"

The waitress, a Black woman with kinky curls, comes over and my father orders his food—three sunny-side-up eggs and wheat toast.

I keep talking. "I was the one that went to the morgue. I mean . . . Mom and his mom were there, but they couldn't go in to identify the body. For Mom, maybe it was this thought that she'd somehow see my face instead of Javion's or that we were kind of the same person to her . . . I'd never seen a friend's dead body before. Since then, it was kind of like I was drunk with that version of his face or I'd see it when I closed my eyes in the shower. I couldn't stop screaming when I got to the church because I didn't realize it'd be a closed-casket funeral."

I went home after the funeral. After all of my friends cleared away from our house, my mother and Javion's mother sat down at our dining room table with me. They brought out a bottle of whiskey and three glasses with ice cubes. Javion's mother's eyes were swollen and red from the day. My mother took down her hair and her hat. We sat in silence for a while as I started to drink, then my mother told a story that started with, "Your father was a beautiful and terrible man, too strong to let love go and too proud to do the right thing."

I look at my father in the diner, lean a bit closer, and say. "At some point, I realized I couldn't separate Javion from you because you left too. I never got to ask for your help with algebra or have you walk me to school. And what about all the other little, important stuff. Did that ever bother you?"

What I couldn't say out loud was that knowing Javion made the abandonment of not having a father more bearable. Or maybe, living for him after he'd died had made it easier. Until that photograph. I knew it was impossible to say everything to my father. What matters most is that you say the first thing. The gargantuan and looming thing that would kill me if I didn't say it.

His food arrives with steam rising off of the eggs. He picks up his utensils and starts to eat. He's either so hungry or so proud that he doesn't look up, but he eats and eats until the plate is done. Then he drinks his water in one drawn-out gulp. He crosses his arms, then stares out the window. The street outside apparently captivates him.

I scoff and say, "I hope you know you're paying. I—"

"I didn't graduate high school," he cut in. "Hell, half of the time, I wasn't even in school. Everybody was fucking poor. Your uncles and I would pickpocket tourists. Chat a white woman up, flirt with her, and someone else gets a hold of her purse. A million different ways to get some change. The only math I knew was how much money I needed to help my mother, to try to be a man. There was no time for feelings."

I exhale, sip coffee, then water, and try to stop my jaw from tightening up.

"Feelings," I say and nod. "Feelings."

"The world does not play nice."

"I'm not talking about the world playing nice," I snap. "I'm talking about the fact that you dated a woman. You fucked her. She had a kid and you left. You left her and you left me."

"I—"

I shoot up from my seat and throw twenty dollars on the table. In no time, I find myself outside, across the street. Everything is too bright. I am sweating. My throat feels like it is closing up. It's getting hard to breathe, to even look forward.

"I'm so fucking stupid. I'm so fucking stupid."

I bury my face in my hands and feel the well inside of me overflowing. I know that if I cry now, I may never stop crying. I realize I've arrived at the precipice and peered too far over the edge, so I think of a good moment. Javion and I were sitting in his backyard. His mother, a nurse, had gone away for the weekend to attend a conference in another city. Javion and I had spent the entire day playing video games and eating baked pizza. Even though I was seventeen and well aware that so many things were going wrong, I couldn't shake feeling grateful. My best friend was sitting next to me with a blunt between his fingers and laughing as he made shitty jokes about different teachers in our school. His laughter felt like looking out at a quiet sea.

Then Javion peered at me for a long and quiet moment. Finally, I looked back at him.

"I've always had a question to ask you," he said, then passed the blunt.

"You're a nosy ass anyway, so you might as well ask."

Another silence followed. Javion shoved his hands into the pockets of his black hoodie and then looked out over the backyard. Then he sighed.

"I'm not asking this because I care what the answer is for real. And I'm not . . . I'm not trying to say anything by asking this. Are you bi or are you gay? I mean . . ."

I sat up a little bit more, took a long puff, and tried not to cough as I pushed the marijuana haze outward. The high placed me in my body in a way that I hated. In my mind, I could quantify a million things. I could find an excuse to go to the bathroom, stare at myself in the mirror, and come up with a solution. Instead, my body fought me. I stared back at him.

"Are you worried about something?"

"Come on," he said as his face twisted into a grimace. "Shit, you always do this. I'm not mad. I'm not worried. I'm asking you a direct question. Give me the damn blunt."

I tried to think of what to say, but the more I thought, the more everything seemed pretty fucking dumb. I spoke anyway.

"Last year was hard. You remember. Ricky got locked up and everyone was acting like they knew him. Daquan and I were so mad about it, then he . . ." I had to stop short and exhale because every time I started to think about it, my head felt like it was floating away from me. Like someone was grabbing some part of me by the throat and pulling it toward the sky.

"I think Daquan and Ricky had something going on. After Ricky went to prison, I was talking to him at a party and he just kissed me. I didn't mind. I—I maybe had thoughts about something like that before, but it wasn't until then that I realized I didn't mind. I felt like something good had happened."

"But . . ." Javion retorted.

I looked at him and smiled. "But Daquan is a fucking dick."

I couldn't remember when the laughing started and us rolling around the floor clutching our stomachs stopped. It was sweat-inducing. It was clumsy, but I felt infinitely loved and seen. When it was over, we sat on the grass after trying to find the remainder of the blunt wherever I'd dropped it. After finishing it, he looked at me again.

"But what about the summer?"

I scoffed and hugged my knees.

"Fuck, dude."

"What?"

"Come on, Javion. You can't be trying to know all my secrets at the same time. It's crass."

He nudged me in the shoulder and said, "I don't know what the fuck that last word means, but it better mean that I'm observant and I noticed when you left last summer, you were acting sketchy as hell. I knew some shit had gone down, but not what."

I stared at him again, but for longer this time. I kept noticing all the reasons that he was beautiful—the indented scar beneath his left eye, the way he never tried to avoid eye contact with me, and the soft dip between his eyebrows whenever he was concerned. Javion hated it, but he wore his emotions like skin. I buried my face in my hands and started to sob. It was a big, brilliant, and ugly thing. I could feel his hands on my shoulders. I could hear Javion talking to me, but even through my choked breaths, I tried to tell him. I tried to tell him everything.

At the camp last summer, some of the kids were strapped down to tables and whatever they'd do to them, you could hear them scream. Sometimes fourteen years old. Sometimes nineteen. Some stayed because they thought they needed it. It wasn't hell. It was a kind of hell. A reworking of it.

When I was over telling him what I could pull out of myself, he sat in front of me on his knees. A sour look was etched onto his face.

"And you don't hate Daquan for snitching on you?"

I just stared back at Javion and didn't answer.

"And your mom for sending you there?"

"Part of me feels like it was my mom and my dad."

His look turned slow and dark. His father had been dead his entire life, a sort of fact and a sort of wound. I'd never exactly told him that my father was dead, but it didn't help that I'd never clarified when he'd said things like, "Dead Daddy Club is meeting up." For a while, he didn't cry exactly. His face got darker and darker, then he started to nod profusely.

He mumbled a few words before going into the house and returning with a bottle of rum from his mother's stash. He didn't need to say anything else because I could feel the unrestrained love in everything that he did. The way he sat so close to me. The way he put his hand on my shoulder and squeezed the flesh there softly. That night he got drunker and angrier than me, rattling off about all of the things that we'd do in college before grabbing my shoulder again and spitting out the words.

"I love you. You're my brother."

That's when I realized it, that sometimes love means being a vessel for somebody else's pain. Not because love should mean taking on someone else's pain, but rather that love makes certain kinds of pain more bearable and teaches us more than the love, the violence, and the story that birthed us. Love can makes us people with wings.

■ ■ ■

On the day of his funeral, the sky was emptied of clouds. Every-thing above was an unforgiving and dying blue. The night before, I drank too much with Keandra, a girl in my grade that I was pretty sure had loved Javion. She and Javion planned to go to prom together. She and I stared at her closet, bewildered. She'd called me over because she didn't know what to wear. The next day my head pounded as we sat in the church pew, half because I'd been screaming and half because we were both pulsating with sickness. It wasn't until we were all outside after the wake that I looked over to see Daquan hugging my mother yards away.

I laugh as I stand across the street from the diner thinking of that moment. Grabbing Daquan by the collar and flinging him into the ground. Screaming a kind of murder, a different murder than what had taken Javion's life, and I buried my fists into Daquan's face as many times as I could. Even if it was just this one public act of brutality, I wanted to be an army of de-struction too. My mother tried to grab me, tried to scream, but something inside of me had exploded. Keandra pulled me away and drove us off. I cried with my face and bloody hands pressed against her car's dashboard. Javion had said it that drunken night in his backyard, "Don't you want revenge?"

I didn't have the heart to admit it at the time, but I did want revenge. Revenge for the fact that he was frozen in my mind in such a grotesque way from what I'd seen of him in the morgue. For everyone else, he could die as the most loved version of him-self. It was me and only me who had been robbed of that luxury.

Do you ever just wish you could erase it? I wanted to ask my father. Do you ever want more than the worst image of someone in your head? Did you ever want a different last image of me?

"You good now?"

I nearly jump from his voice near me. It's my father smoking a cigarette. He offers me one. Then we sit on the curb. It takes a few moments of silence from me to realize what I need to say.

I start to talk. "I didn't arrange to meet you because I wanted some happy ending or relationship. I know how these things go and I know how men are. I think men can do more than take from the people that we love or disappear or not have answers to really important questions."

I reach into my tote bag and pull out a stack of folded papers. Some papers are dog-eared, stained, or faded, and others are newer.

"What's this?" he asks as I hand them to him.

"When I was five, Ma sat me down and told me about you. And you know, I was so excited because the memory of you moved her."

I finish my cigarette, so he hands me another after lighting it for me. Ahead of us and above us, the sky is beginning to turn a slight burnt orange.

"She asked me to write a letter that she'd send to you. So I wrote one and she sent it, but you never wrote back. I—"

"I don't think—" he starts to say.

I cut him a harsh look and snap, "I don't need you to talk right now. I need you to listen."

"Alright. Alright," he replies softly, "I'm listening."

I started writing letters to him again in the third grade when I tried out for the basketball team, but wasn't selected. I returned home grumpy, had a fight with my mother who was upset with my mood, and was sent to my room. I thought of my father and started to write. Those letters, in part, helped me cope with school suspensions, friends moving away, fights with my brother, the nerves of going off to college, and the first time a boy picked me up from my house in the middle of the night because he wanted to see me. They'd only stopped for a short time after Javion's death. Then the letters turned into my way of writing to him.

"It's kind of how I started writing," I say. "I wanted to make you understand what you missed out on. Because at some point, I realized that one of the best ways we can love people is to not be afraid of them."

My father stares at a letter on top of the stack, the one I wrote about learning to drive. His eyes fixed on a particular section of the page. He started to nod slowly.

"I don't know why you didn't stick around, but I knew that if it was possible, I had to tell you that you helped me. I don't think it's good enough or makes what you did any better, but somehow I found a way for you to help me. To love people, you gotta to be willing to live and share their reality with them."

My phone rings. I don't have to look at it to know who it is. My father holds the letters to his chest.

"I've got to go. There's somebody picking me up. I only had a half an hour to do this," I tell him.

I stand. So he stands as well. Now I realize that we are the same exact height and build—two wiry frames with probing eyes and big lips. This time, he looks at me with a bit of sadness; an emotion a world away from the strong certainty that he gave off earlier.

"Here," he says as he takes my hand and puts a worn journal in it. Even with the book passed onto me, he holds my hand.

"I know who I am and I know that maybe I wasn't meant to be your father. And I can't speak for whether or not I'm proud of you because I don't know you, but there is one thing that I can tell you from the good part of me."

"What is that?" I asked.

"If God is in you, God is in me too."

He pulls me in fast. For an ephemeral moment, I am sure that the hug will last forever. His arms are strong around me. I close my eyes and breathe in his scent; a mixture of dirt and sweat and medium-grade cologne. Then he is gone. Walking away until I realize the blur in my vision that swallowed him up was just my quiet crying.

■ ■ ■

My friend, Bem, is cognizant of what I was actually trying to say when I playfully asked him to pull over so we could go into a bar. I exit the car and say, "You know what? Maybe I'll just hang out here for another day or two."

I drink too much whiskey by the time I miss my flight that evening.

In the previous weeks, I'd slowed down on drinking. Not because I thought I had a problem, but I was worried that the mysticism it gave life was too easy to fall into. I started writing more on the weekends and pinning story ideas to a giant cork board on my wall. I was convinced that the beginnings of a novel were brewing inside of me until I read a section of it to a writer friend. The friend looked at me and said deadpan, "You've got to stop writing about your missing father."

I felt like a ghost. A fool. I thought of all of the open mics or spoken word events that I'd shared poetry at. I thought of all the positive feedback that people gave me. No matter the audience's ethnicity, at least one person would come up to me crying and telling me that something about what I'd written was so sad.

Sometimes I had to say back, "But that was one of my happy pieces."

I had a fear that my work was stuck in a gray area. No longer the weird trappings of teenage creative therapy sessions on paper and not quite the literary and poetic gold that I ached to produce. Could it even be called art if it was some obsessive thing that kept crawling back into your lap, oozing all over you, and begging you to give it more?

"I always felt like the part of me that wanted to write was monstrous," I say to Bem after my sixth whiskey on the rocks. "It always seemed twisted that that was the most reliable place that I could go to. The sad Black gay boy longing for a man to teach him how to live."

"But that's normal. We all put parts of ourselves in what we write," Bem replies.

I want to scoff at him, but couldn't help but smile when he reaches for my hand and squeezes it. I am always set ablaze by how vivid his kindness was. It's a strange side effect of being gay that I could both long for a man to be nice to me while also knowing that affection came in a billion shades. I pull my hand from his after a few moments, then press my face against the bar.

The bar is large and wooden with a sunken area for more tables and chairs. I like the way the dying light of the Arizona evening floods in through the windows. I like that the jukebox only plays five songs, my favorite of them being "Stand By Your Man," which made me want to fall in love all over again. I like that the bartender is a really old white man that never speaks to us, but keeps eavesdropping.

I lift my head off of the cool bar and take a deep breath while stirring the straw in my cup.

"It's how I learned to love writing though. Those letters were how I figured out that words were important to me. Isn't that fucked up?"

Bem nudges me on the shoulder playfully, then speaks, "My favorite line of yours that I've heard or read was—"

"Noooooo!" I groan as I try to cover my ears before deciding to have the courage to sit up and stare at him. "Go ahead. I like your non-literary brain giving me literary praise."

"'Now I, fatherless in/two ways, marvel at the lulling spaces/between this skeleton's ribs./My mother calls me/from downstairs.'"

"'Always time to leave,'" I finish the line for Bem, then ask, "Are you sure you're not gay?"

Bem sips his drink and laughs. "Don't you always say everyone's a little gay?"

I laugh, then the bar's front doors fly open and a parade of white women wearing purple sashes and dick hats storm in, one woman already latching onto another's shoulder. A brunette slaps her card down on the counter. Bem and I stare at each other. The bartender exchanges a knowing look with us.

Bem decides to pay the tab. I stumbled out of the bar. Bem is talking about getting nachos, how I can sleep in his bed to nurse off the drunk once we get back to his house, but I can't register anything he says.

The sky is still as orange as it was earlier. A flock of birds moves over the bar and I stare at the building, wooden and dark and shining.

"He had a brother," I mutter.

Bem's keys stop jingling as he puts them in the ignition.

"What?"

I lean back against my seat and fondle the journal in my hand. I think of Javion stumbling off to sleep after that drunken night in his yard, how we woke up sweating and staring at each other's bed head. We laughed like goons as daybreak washed over us. I realize that I miss laughing with him because it weighed me down. It moved through my chest. Sometimes it still moves through my chest.

"It's what he gave me. He had a brother named Cedric. Died in some horrible way. Reading his journal set him straight."

As I fall asleep, I can only think of one thing. Bem turns on the radio. The singer croons on, his voice sounding like the sea. The song changes me, like a chemical reaction. He haunts me with his words, "Who am I? Who am I? Who am I?" For once in my life, I feel like I can decide the answer for myself.

We pull away with the sky so huge and unnameable that I become a child as I melt into my seat. I decide this place will be the opening scene of whatever book I write next. It will be a bestseller, a meditation on unmangled love, an act of revenge. I decide that I will be a star.

Acknowledgments

I wrote this memoir because, at some point, I feared I would always be the boy grappling for a father who had done wrong. Through writing, I confronted this fallacy and came out the other end, a little more realized and grateful for my body, my heart, my mind, and all the people who loved me and asked questions. I want to acknowledge the twelve-year-old boy who was assigned to write a short story and started a new life with his pen. Many parts of this book challenged me to have the courage to make sense of a complicated life as best as I could. So many people believe that young, Black people don't have stories to tell, but this book proves that we do.

I'd like to acknowledge the writers that fed so much into me as I wrote this book: James Baldwin, Saidiya Hartman, Jesmyn Ward, Kiese Laymon, Ocean Vuong, Malcolm X, Huey P. Newton, Alexander Chee, Angela Davis, Jamal Joseph, Essex Hemphill, André Aciman. Without so many of their works, many writers would be spinning around in unorchestrated chaos, instead of being committed to a legacy. I also wouldn't be the writer I am without the love of and support of friends, like Bobby Luck, Kell Oliver, Alli Maloney, Madeline ffitch, Rayji de Guia, Allison Amend, Manan Kapoor, Nikki Elmer, my Columbus community. Special thanks to Nadia Burton for being my friend, family, and first peer to really encourage my writing; to Eli Hiller for showing me that, for some, curiosity and kindness can be infinite; and Camille for reading sweetly from over my shoulder as I wrote new worlds while making a new world with him.

A special thanks to Hanif Abdurraqib for taking a chance on me, a writer fighting to break into an industry that locks so many marginalized writers out, and the Tin House team: Craig Popelars, Masie Cochran, Nanci McCloskey, Becky Kraemer, Jakob Vala, Sangi Lama, Alex Gonzales, Alyssa Ogi, Elizabeth DeMeo, and Diane Chonette. Thank you to RJR News for sharing excerpts of Cedric Murray's diary.

Thank you to the literary agents that helped me bring this book to fruition, most notably Elle McKenzie for countless hours of editing with me through 2020, and Samantha Haywood and Chelene Knight for easing my anxieties through the debut process. I'm grateful for the variety of spaces I've been able to workshop and write this book, ranging from residencies with Sangam House, Studios of Key West, Norton Island, La Maison Baldwin, Under The Volcano, Hurston/Wright Foundation, and comfort places, like a small desk in Saint-Denis to the rooftop of Funky Fes Hostel in Morocco.